# The
# Believer's
# Secret
## of the Master's
# Indwelling

# The Believer's Secret of the Master's Indwelling

## ANDREW MURRAY

## BETHANY HOUSE PUBLISHERS

MINNEAPOLIS, MINNESOTA 55438

A Division of Bethany Fellowship, Inc.

Originally titled *The Master's Indwelling*

Copyright © 1977
Bethany House Publishers
All Rights Reserved

Published by Bethany House Publishers
A Division of Bethany Fellowship, Inc.
6820 Auto Club Road, Minneapolis, Minnesota 55438

Printed in the United States of America

**Library of Congress Cataloging-in-Publication Data**

Murray, Andrew, 1828-1917.
    The believer's secret of the Master's indwelling.

    (The Andrew Murray Christian maturity library)
    Previously published as: The Master's indwelling.
I. Christian life.  I. Title.  II. Series: Murray, Andrew, 1828-
1917. Andrew Murray Christian maturity library.
BV4501.2.M87      1986      248.4      86-6814
ISBN 0-87123-653-2 (pbk.)

# Contents

# 1

## Carnal Christians

*1 Corinthians 3:1—And I, brethren, could not speak unto you as unto spiritual, but as unto carnal.*

The apostle here speaks of two stages of the Christian life, two types of Christians: "I could not speak unto you as unto *spiritual*, but as unto *carnal*, even as unto babes in Christ." They were Christians in Christ, but instead of being spiritual Christians, they were carnal. "I have fed you with milk, and not with meat: for hitherto ye were not able to bear it, neither yet are ye able, for ye are yet *carnal*." Here is that word a second time. "For whereas"—this is the proof—"there is among you envying, and strife, and divisions, are ye not carnal, and walk as men? For while one saith, I am of Paul; and another, I am of Apollos; are ye not carnal?" Four times the apostle uses the word carnal.

In the wisdom which the Holy Spirit gives him, Paul feels that he cannot write to the Corinthian Christians unless he knows their state and unless he tells them of it. If he gives spiritual food to men who are carnal Christians, he is doing them more harm than good, for they are not fit to take it. He cannot feed them with meat; he must feed them with milk. And so he tells them at the very outset of the epistle what he sees to be their state.

In the two previous chapters Paul had spoken about his ministry being by the Holy Spirit; now he begins to tell them what must be the state of a people in order to accept spiritual truth: "I have not liberty to speak to you as I would, for you are carnal, and you cannot receive spiritual truth." That suggests to us the solemn thought that in the church of Christ there are two classes of Christians: (1) Those who have lived many years as believers and yet always remain babes; (2) Those who are spiritual men because they have given themselves up to the power and the leading of the Holy Spirit—i.e., to His entire rule. If we are to obtain a blessing, we must first decide to which of these classes we belong. Are we, by the grace of God, in deep humility living a spiritual life, or are we living a carnal life? Then, let us first try to understand what is meant by the carnal state in which believers may be living.

From what we find in Corinthians, we notice four marks of the carnal state. First, it is simply a condition of protracted infancy. For example, if we see a beautiful six-month-old baby who cannot speak or walk, we do not trouble ourselves about that; it is natural and ought to be so. But suppose a year later we find that the child has not grown at all, and three years later there is still no growth. Then we would say: "There must be some terrible disease"; and the baby who at six months old brought such joy to everyone who saw him now has become to the mother and to all a source of anxiety and sorrow. There is something wrong; the child cannot grow. At six months old it was quite right that it should eat nothing but milk; but years have passed by, and it remains in the same weakly state.

Now this is just the condition of many believers. They are converted; they know what it is to have assurance and faith; they believe in pardon for sin; they begin to work for God; and yet, somehow, there is very little growth in spirituality, in the real heavenly life. We come into contact with them, and we feel at once there is something lacking; there is none of the beauty of holiness or of the power of God's Spirit in them. This is the condition of the carnal

*[handwritten margin note: 1. No Growth after Conversion]*

Corinthians, expressed in what was said to the Hebrews: "You have had the gospel so long that by this time you ought to be teachers, and yet you need that men should teach you the very rudiments of the oracles of God." Isn't it sad to see a believer who has been converted five, ten, or twenty years and yet shows no growth, no strength, and no joy of holiness?

What are the marks of a little child? One is that a little child cannot help himself. He is always keeping others occupied serving him. What a tyrant a baby in a house often is! The mother cannot go out, there must be a servant to nurse it; it needs to be cared for constantly. God made a man to care for others, but the baby was made to be cared for and to be helped. So there are Christians who always want help. Their pastor and their Christian friends must always be teaching and comforting them. They go to church, to prayer meetings, and to conventions—always wanting to be helped. This is a sign of spiritual infancy.

The other sign of an infant is this: he can do nothing to help his fellowman. Every man is expected to contribute something to the welfare of society. Everyone has a place to fill and a work to do, but the babe can do nothing for the commonwealth. It is just so with Christians. How little some can do! They take a part in work, as it is called, but there is little exercising of spiritual power and carrying real blessing. Should we not each ask, "Have I outgrown my spiritual infancy?" Some must reply, "No, instead of having gone forward, I have gone backward, and the joy of conversion and the first love is gone." Alas! They are babes in Christ; they are yet carnal.

The second mark of the carnal state is this: there is sin and failure continually. Paul says, "Whereas there is among you envying, and strife, and division, are ye not carnal?" A man gives way to temper. He may be a minister, or a preacher of the gospel, or a Sunday school teacher, and most earnest at the prayer meeting, yet he often shows strife or bitterness or envying. Alas! In Galatians 5:20 we are told that hatred and envy are especially the works of the flesh. How often among Christians who have to work together do we see divisions and bitterness! May God have mercy upon them because the fruit of the Spirit, which is love, is so frequently absent from His own people.

You ask, "Why is it that for twenty years I have been fighting with my temper and cannot conquer it?" It is because you have not been fighting with the *root* of the

*2. Sin continues to reign*

temper. You have not seen that it is because you are in the carnal state and have not properly yielded to the Spirit of God. It may be that you never were taught it; that you never saw it in God's Word; that you never believed it. But there it is; the truth of God remains unchangeable. Jesus Christ can give us the victory over sin and can keep us from actual transgression. I am not telling you that the root of sin will be eradicated and that you no longer will have any natural tendency to sin. When the Holy Spirit comes with His power for service as a gift, He comes in divine grace to fill the heart. Then there is victory over sin and power not to fulfill the lusts of the flesh.

You see a mark of the carnal state not only in unlovingness, self-consciousness and bitterness, but in so many other sins. How much worldliness, how much ambition among men, how much seeking for the honor that comes from man—all the fruit of the carnal life—to be found in the midst of Christian activity! Let us remember that the carnal state is a state of continual sinning and failure, and God wants us not only to make confession of individual sins, but also to come to the acknowledgment that they are the sign that we are not living a healthy life—we are yet carnal.

A **third mark** is that this carnal state

3. Graces of the Spirit have not been gained

may be found in existence in connection with great spiritual gifts. There is a difference between gifts and graces. The graces of the Spirit are humility and love, like the humility and love of Christ. The graces of the Spirit are to make a man free from self; the gifts of the Spirit are to fit a man for work. We see this illustrated among the Corinthians. In the first chapter Paul says, "I thank God . . . that in everything ye are enriched by him in all utterance, and in all knowledge." In the 12th and 14th chapters we see that the gifts of prophecy and of working miracles were in great power among them; but the graces of the Spirit were noticeably absent.

We may find this in our days as well as in the time of the Corinthians. I may be a minister of the gospel; I may teach God's Word beautifully; I may have influence and gather a large congregation, and yet, alas! I may be a carnal man, a man who may be used by God, and a blessing to others, and yet marked by the carnal life.

You all know the law that a thing is named according to its most prominent characteristic. Now, in these carnal Corinthians there was a little of God's Spirit but the flesh predominated; the Spirit did not rule their whole life. On the other hand,

14

the spiritual men were not called so because
there was no flesh in them but because the
Spirit in them had obtained dominance,
and when one met them and had conversation with them, one felt that the Spirit of
God had sanctified them.

Ah, let us beware lest the blessing God
gives us in our work deceive us and lead
us to think that because He has blessed
us, we must be spiritual men. God may
give us gifts that we use, and yet our lives
may not be wholly in the power of the Holy
Spirit.

The fourth mark of the carnal state is
a man's inability to receive spiritual truths.
That is what the apostle writes to the Corinthians, "I could not preach to you as unto
spiritual; you are not fit for spiritual truth
after being Christians so long; you cannot
yet bear it; I have to feed you with milk."
I am afraid that in the church of the nine-
teenth century we often make a terrible
mistake. We have a congregation in which
the majority are carnal men. We give these
men spiritual teaching, and they admire
it, and understand it, and rejoice in such
ministry; yet their lives are not practically
affected. They work for Christ in a certain
way, but we can scarcely recognize the true
sanctification of the Spirit; we dare not say
they are spiritual men, full of the Holy Spirit.

4. Inability
to
understand
God's
truths

Now, let us recognize this with regard to ourselves. A man may become very earnest, may take in all the teaching he hears; he may be able to discern, for discernment is a gift. He may say, "That man helps me in this line, and that man in another direction, and a third man is remarkable for another gift"; yet all the time the carnal life may be living strongly in him, and when he gets into trouble with some friend, or Christian worker, or worldly man, the carnal root is bearing its terrible fruit, and the spiritual food has failed to enter his heart. Beware of that. Mark the Corinthians and learn from them. Paul did not say to them, "You cannot bear the truth as I would speak it to you," because they were ignorant or a stupid people. The Corinthians prided themselves on their wisdom and sought it above everything, Paul said, "I thank God that you are enriched in utterance, in knowledge, and in wisdom; nevertheless, you are yet carnal, your life is not holy; your life is not sanctified unto the humility of the life of the Lamb of God. You cannot yet take in real spiritual truth."

We find the carnal state not only at Corinth, but also throughout the Christian world today. Many Christians are asking, "Why is there such feebleness in the Church?" We cannot ask this question too earnestly, and I trust that God himself will so impress it upon our hearts that we shall say to Him, "It must be changed. Have mercy upon us." But, ah! that prayer and that change cannot come until we have begun to see that there is a carnal root ruling in believers; they are living more after the flesh than after the Spirit; they are yet carnal Christians.

Let us consider the passage "from carnal to spiritual." Did Paul find any spiritual believers? Undoubtedly he did. Just read the 6th chapter of the Epistle to the Galatians! That was a church where strife, bitterness, and envy were ripe. But the apostle says in the first verse: "Brethren, if a man be overtaken in a fault, ye which are spiritual restore such an one in the spirit of meekness." Here we see that the marks of the spiritual man are meekness, power, and love to help and restore those that are fallen. The carnal man cannot do that. If there is a true spiritual life that can be lived, the great question is: Is the way open, and how can I enter into the spiritual state? Here, again, I have four short answers.

First, we must know that there is such a spiritual life to be lived by men on earth. Nothing cuts the roots of the Christian life so much as unbelief. People do not believe what God has said about what He is willing to do for His children. Men do not believe

that when God says, "Be filled with the
Spirit," He means it for every Christian.
And yet Paul wrote to the Ephesians, to
each one, "Be filled with the Spirit, and
do not be drunk with wine." Just as little
as you may be drunk with wine, so little
may you live without being filled with the
Spirit. Now, if God means that this life is
for believers, then the first thing we need
to do is to study and to believe God's Word
until in faith our hearts are filled with the
assurance that there is such a life possible,
which it is our duty to live, and that we
*can* be spiritual men. God's Word teaches
us that God does not expect a man to live
as he ought for one minute unless the Holy
Spirit is in him to enable him to do it.

We do not want the Holy Spirit only
when we preach, or when we have some
special temptation of the devil to meet, or
some great burden to bear. God says, "My
child cannot live a right life unless he is
guided by my Spirit every minute." That is
the mark of the child of God: "As many as
are led by the Spirit of God, they are the
sons of God." In Romans 5 we read, "The
love of God is shed abroad in our hearts
by the Holy Spirit which is given unto us."
That is to be the common, everyday experience of the believer, not his life at set
times only. Did ever a father or mother

think, "For today I want my child to love me"? No, they expect the love every day.

So God wants His child every moment to have a heart filled with love of the Spirit. In the eyes of God, it is most unnatural to expect a man to love as he should if he is not filled with the Spirit. Oh, let us believe a man *can* be a spiritual man. Thank God, there is now the blessing waiting us. "Be filled with the Spirit." "Be led by the Spirit." There *is* the blessing. If you have to say, "O God, I have not this blessing," say it; but say also, "Lord, I know it is my duty, my solemn obligation, to have it, for without it I cannot live in perfect peace with Thee all the day; without it I cannot glorify Thee and do the work Thou wouldst have me do." This is our first step from the carnal to the spiritual—to recognize that a spiritual life, a walk in the Spirit, is within our reach. How can we ask God to guide us into spiritual life if we have not a clear, confident conviction that there is such a life to be had?

Then comes the second step: A man must see the shame and guilt of his not having lived such a life. Some people admit there is a spiritual life to live, and that they have not lived it. They feel sorry for themselves, and pity themselves, and think, "How sad that I am too feeble for it! How sad that God gives it to others, but has not given it to me!" They have great compassion for themselves instead of saying, "Alas! it has been our unfaithfulness, our unbelief, our disobedience that has kept us from giving ourselves utterly to God. We have to blush and to be ashamed before God because we do not live as spiritual men."

A man does not get converted without having conviction of sin. When that conviction of sin comes and his eyes are opened, he learns to be afraid of his sin, and to flee from it to Christ, and to accept Christ as a mighty deliverer. However, a man needs a second conviction of sin—that is, a believer must be convicted of his particular sin. The sins of an unconverted man are different from the sins of a believer. For instance, an unconverted man is not ordinarily convicted of the corruption of his nature. He thinks principally about external sins: "I have sworn, been a liar, and I am on the way to hell." He is then convicted for conversion. But the believer is in quite a different condition. His sins are far more blamable, for he has had the light and the love and the Spirit of God given to him. His sins are far deeper. He has striven to conquer them, but he has grown to see that his nature is utterly corrupt, that the carnal mind, the flesh, within him is making his whole state utterly wretched. When a believer is thus convicted by the Holy Spirit, it is especially his life of unbelief that condemns him, because he sees that the great guilt connected with this has kept him from receiving the full gift of God's Holy Spirit. He is brought down in shame and confusion of face, and he begins to cry, "Woe is me, for I am undone. I have heard of God by the hearing of the ear; I have known a great deal of Him and preached about Him, but now mine eye seeth Him!" God comes near him. Job, the righteous man, whom God trusted, saw in himself the deep sin of self and its righteousness that he had never seen before. Until this conviction of the wrongness of our carnal state as believers comes to each one of us; until we are willing to get this conviction from God, to take time before God to be humbled and convicted, we never can become spiritual men.

Then comes the third mark, which is only one step out of the carnal state into the spiritual. One step. Oh, that is a blessed message I bring to you—it is only one step. I know many people will refuse to admit that it is only one step; they think it too little for such a mighty change. But was not conversion only one step?

*[margin note:]* Indeed !

*[margin note:]* 3. Breaking with the flesh

So it is when a man passes from the carnal to the spiritual. You ask if when I talk of a spiritual man I am not thinking of a man of spiritual maturity, a real saint, and you say, "Does that come in one day? Is there no growth in holiness?" I reply that spiritual maturity cannot come in a day. We cannot expect it. It takes growth until the whole beauty of the image of Christ is formed in a man. But still I say that it needs but one step for a man to get out of the carnal life into the spiritual life. It is when a man utterly breaks with the flesh, when he gives up the flesh into the crucifixion death of Christ, when he sees that everything about it is accursed and that he cannot deliver himself from it, and then claims the slaying power of Christ's cross within him. When a man does this and says, "This spiritual life prepared for me is the free gift of my God in Christ Jesus," he understands how one step can bring him out of the carnal into the spiritual state.

In that spiritual life there will be much still to be learned. There will still be imperfections. Spiritual life is not perfect; but the predominant characteristic will be spiritual. When a man has given himself up to the real, living, acting, ruling power of God's Spirit, he has come into the right position in which he can grow. You never think of growing out of sickness into health. You may grow out of feebleness into strength, as a baby grows to be a strong man; but where there is disease, there must come healing if a cure is to be effected. There are Christians who think that they must grow out of the carnal state into the spiritual state. You never can. What could help those carnal Corinthians? To give them milk could not help them, for milk was a proof they were in the wrong state. To give them meat would not help them, for they were unfit to eat it. What they needed was the knife of the surgeon. Paul says that the carnal life must be cut out. "They that are Christ's have crucified the flesh." When a man understands what that means, and accepts it in the faith of what Christ can do, then one step can bring him from the carnal to the spiritual. One simple act of faith in the power of Christ's death, one act of surrender to the fellowship of Christ's death, trusting the Holy Spirit to make it ours, will make it ours, will bring deliverance from the power of our efforts.

What brought deliverance to that poor condemned sinner who was most dark and wretched in his unconverted state? He felt he could do nothing good of himself. What did he do? He saw set before him the almighty Saviour and he cast himself into

His arms; he trusted himself to that omnipotent love and cried, "Lord, have mercy
upon me." That was salvation. It was not
for what he did that Christ accepted him.
Oh, believers, if any of us who are conscious
that the carnal state predominates have to
say, "It marks me: I am a religious man,
an earnest man, a friend of missions: I
work for Christ in my church, but, alas!
temper and sin and worldliness have still
the mastery over my soul," hear the word
of God. If any will come and say, "I have
struggled, I have prayed, I have wept, and
it has not helped me," then he must do
one other thing. He must see that the living
Christ is God's provision for his holy, spiritual life. He must believe that the Christ
who accepted him once, at conversion, in
His wonderful love is now waiting to say
to him that he may become a spiritual man,
entirely given up to God. If he will believe
that, his fear will vanish and he will say,
"It can be done; if Christ will accept and
take charge, it shall be done."

Finally, my last mark. A man must take
that step, a solemn but blessed step. It cost
some of you five or ten years before you
took the step of conversion. You wept and
prayed for years and could not find peace
until you took that step. So, in the spiritual
life, you may go to teacher after teacher

and say, "Tell me about the spiritual life, the baptism of the Spirit and holiness," and yet you may remain just where you were. Many of us would love to have sin taken away. Who loves to have a hasty temper? Who loves to have a proud disposition? Who loves to have a worldly heart? No one. We go to Christ to take it away, and He does not do it; and we ask, "Why will He not do it? I have prayed very earnestly." It is because you wanted Him to take away the ugly fruits while the poisonous root stayed in you. You did not ask Him to nail the flesh to His cross, and that you should henceforth give up self entirely to the power of His Spirit.

There is deliverance, but not in the way we seek it. Suppose a painter had a piece of canvas on which he desired to work out some beautiful picture. Suppose that piece of canvas does not belong to him, and anyone has a right to take it and to use it for any other purpose. Do you think the painter would bestow much work on that? No. Yet people want Jesus Christ to bestow His trouble upon them by taking away this temper or that other sin, though in their hearts they have not yielded themselves utterly to His command and His keeping. It cannot be. But if you will come and give your whole life into His charge, Christ Jesus is mighty to save; Christ Jesus waits to be gracious; Christ Jesus waits to fill you with His Spirit.

Will you not take the step? God grant that we may be led by His Spirit to yield ourselves to Him as never before. Will you not come humbly, confessing that the carnal life has predominated too much, has altogether marked you, and that you have a bitter consciousness that with all the blessing God has bestowed, He has not made you what you want to be—a spiritual man? *It is the Holy Spirit alone who by His indwelling can make a spiritual man.*

Come then and cast yourself at God's feet, with this one thought, "Lord, I give myself, an empty vessel, to be filled with Thy Spirit." Every day each one of you sees at the tea table an empty cup set there, waiting to be filled with tea when the proper time comes. So with every dish, every plate. They are cleansed and empty, ready to be filled. Emptied and cleansed. Oh, come! And just as a vessel is set apart to receive what it is to contain, say to Christ you desire from this hour to be a vessel set apart to be filled with His Spirit, given up to be a spiritual man. Bow down in the deepest emptiness of soul and say, "O God, I have nothing!" And then surely as you place yourself before Him you have a right to say, "My God will fulfill His promise! I claim from Him the filling of the Holy Spirit to make me a spiritual, instead of a carnal, Christian." If you place yourself at His feet and tarry there; if you abide in that humble surrender and that childlike trust, as sure as God lives the blessing *will* come.

Oh, should we not bow in shame before God as we think of His whole church and see so much of the carnal prevailing? Should we not bow in shame before God as we think of all the carnality in our hearts and lives? Then let us bow with great faith in God's mercy. Deliverance is nigh, deliverance is coming, deliverance is waiting, deliverance is sure. Let us trust; God will give it.

## 2

## The Self Life

*Matthew 16:24—If any man will come after me, let him deny himself, and take up his cross, and follow me.*

In the 13th verse we read that Jesus at Caesarea Philippi asked His disciples, "Whom do men say that I the Son of man am?" When they had answered, He asked them, "But whom say ye that I am?" And in verse 16 Peter answered and said, "Thou art the Christ, the Son of the living God." Jesus answered and said unto him, "Blessed art thou, Simon Bar-jona: for flesh and blood hath not revealed it unto thee, but my Father which is in heaven. And I say also unto thee, That thou art Peter, and upon this rock I will build my church; and the gates of hell shall not prevail against it." Then in verse 21 we read how Jesus began to tell His disciples of His approaching death; and in verse 22 how Peter began to rebuke Him, saying, "Be it far from thee, Lord: this shall not be unto thee." But Jesus turned and said unto Peter, "Get thee behind me, Satan: thou art an offence unto me, for thou savourest not the things that be of God, but those that be of men." Then said Jesus unto His disciples, "If any man will come after me, let him deny himself, and take up his cross, and follow me."

We often hear about the life of compromise and the question comes up, What lies at the root of it? Why are so many Christians wasting their lives in terrible bondage to the world instead of living in the manifestation and the privilege and the glory of the child of God? Then perhaps another question comes to us: Why is it that when we see a thing is wrong and strive against it, we cannot conquer it? Why, after praying and vowing a hundred times, are we still living a mingled, divided, halfhearted life? To those questions there is one answer: *Self* is the root of the whole trouble. Therefore, if anyone asks me, "How can I get rid of this life of compromise?" the answer would not be, "You must do this, or that, or the other thing." It would be, "A new life from above, the life of Christ, must take the place of the self-life; then alone can we be conquerors."

We always go from the outward to the inward. Let us do so here; let us consider from these words of the text the one word "self." Jesus said to Peter, "If any man will come after me, let him deny *himself* [his own self], and take up his cross, and follow me." That is the mark of a disciple; that is the secret of the Christian life: deny self and all will come out right. Note that Peter was a believer, a believer who had been taught by the Holy Spirit. He had given an answer that pleased Christ wonderfully: "Thou art the Christ, the Son of the living God." Do not think that that was nothing extraordinary. We learn it in our catechism. Peter did not. But Christ saw that the Holy Spirit of the Father had been teaching him and He said: "Blessed art thou, Simon Barjona." But note how strong the carnal man still is in Peter. Peter could understand about the glory, "Thou art the Son of God"; but when Christ spoke about the cross and the death, he could not understand, and he ventured in his self-confidence to say, "Lord: this shall not be unto thee." In other words, "Thou canst not be crucified and die." And Christ had to rebuke him: "Get thee behind me, Satan. Thou savourest not the things that be of God." Jesus was saying, "You are talking like a mere carnal man, and not as the Spirit of God would teach you." Then He went on to say, "Remember, it is not only I who am to be crucified, but you also; it is not only I who am to die, but you also. If a man would be My disciple, he must deny self, and he must take up his cross and follow Me."

Let us examine this one word "self." It is only as we learn to understand what self is that we really know what is at the root of all our failure and are prepared to go to Christ for deliverance.

Now let us consider, first of all, the nature of this self life, then denote some of its works, and finally, ask the question, "How may we be delivered from it?"

Self is the power with which God has created and endowed every intelligent creature. Self is the very center of a created being. And why did God give the angels or man a self? The object of this self was that we might bring it as an empty vessel unto God that He might put into it His life. God gave me the power of self-determination that I might bring this self every day and say, "O God, work in it. I offer it to thee." God wanted a vessel into which He might pour out His divine fullness of beauty, wisdom and power; and so He created the world, the sun, the moon, the stars, the trees, the flowers, and the grass, which all show forth the riches of His wisdom, beauty, and goodness. But they do it without knowing that they do. Then God created the angels with a self and a will, to see whether they would come and voluntarily yield themselves to Him as vessels for Him to fill. But alas! they did not all do that. There was one at the head of a great company who began to look upon himself and to think of the wonderful powers with which God had endowed him, and to delight in himself. He began to think, "Must such a being as I always remain dependent on God?" He exalted himself, and pride asserted itself in separation from God. At that very moment he became, instead of an angel in heaven, a devil in hell. Self turned to God is the glory of allowing the Creator to reveal himself in us. Self turned away from God is the very darkness and fire of hell.

We all know the terrible result of that action. God created man, and Satan came in the form of a serpent and tempted Eve with the thought of becoming as God, having an independent self, knowing good and evil. And while he spoke with her, he breathed into her, in those words, the very poison and the very pride of hell. His own evil spirit, the very poison of hell, entered humanity, and it is this cursed self that we have inherited from our first parents. It was that self that ruined and brought destruction upon this world. And all that

there has been of sin, of darkness, of wretchedness, and of misery; and all that there
will be throughout the countless ages of
eternity in hell will be nothing but the reign
of self, the curse of self, separating man
and turning him away from his God. And
if we are to understand fully what Christ
is to do for us, and are to become partakers
of a full salvation, we must learn to know,
and to hate, and to give up entirely this
cursed self.

Now, what are the works of self? I
could mention many, but let us take the
simplest forms which we manifest continually: self-will, self-confidence, self-
exaltation.

*Self-will*, pleasing self, is the great sin
of man. It is at the root of all compromising
with the world, which is the ruin of so many.
Men cannot understand why they should
not please themselves and do as they will.
Numbers of Christians have never gotten
hold of the idea that a Christian is a man
who is never to seek his own will, but is
always to seek the will of God, as a man
in whom the very spirit of Christ lives.
"Lo, I come to do Thy will, O my God!"

We find Christians pleasing themselves
in a thousand ways, and yet trying to be
happy, good, and useful; and they do not
know that at the root of it all is self-will

robbing them of the blessing. Christ said to Peter, "Peter, deny yourself." But instead of doing that, Peter said, "I will deny my Lord and not myself." He never said it in those words, but Christ said to him the last night, "Thou shalt deny me," and he did. What was the cause? Self-pleasing. He became afraid when the woman servant charged him with belonging to Jesus, and three times said, "I know not this man, I have nothing to do with Him." He denied Christ. Just think of it! No wonder Peter wept those bitter tears. It was a choice between self—that ugly, cursed self—and Jesus, that beautiful, blessed Son of God. And Peter chose self. No wonder he thought, "Instead of denying myself, I have denied Jesus; what a choice I have made!" No wonder he wept bitterly.

Christians, look at your own lives in the light of the words of Jesus. Do you find self-will, self-pleasing? Remember this: every time you please yourself, you deny Jesus. It is one or the other. You must please Him only and deny self, or you must please yourself and deny Him.

If you please yourself, then will follow *self-confidence*, with its related forms, self-trust, self-effort, self-dependence. What was it that led Peter to deny Jesus? Christ had warned him. Why did he not take warning? Self-confidence. He was so sure, "Lord, I love Thee. For three years I have followed Thee. Lord, I deny that it ever can be. I am ready to go to prison and to death." It was simply self-confidence.

People have often asked me, "Why do I fail? I desire so earnestly and pray so fervently to live in God's will." My answer generally is, "Simply because you trust yourself." But they say, "No, I do not. I know I am not good, and I know that God is willing to keep me. I put my trust in Jesus." But I reply, "No, my brother, no. If you trusted God and Jesus, you could not fall, but you trust yourself."

Do let us believe that the cause of every failure in the Christian life is nothing but this. I trust this cursed self instead of trusting Jesus. I trust my own strength instead of the almighty strength of God. And that is why Christ says, "This self must be denied."

The third form of the works of self is *self-exaltation.* Ah, how much pride and jealousy there is in the Christian world; how much sensitiveness to what men say of us or think of us; how much desire for human praise and pleasing men instead of always living in the presence of God with the one thought: "Am I pleasing to Him?"

Christ said, "How can ye believe who receive honor one of another?" Receiving honor of one another renders a life of faith absolutely impossible. This self started from hell, it separated us from God, it is a cursed deceiver that leads us astray from Jesus.

Finally, what must we do to get rid of it? Jesus answers us in the words of our text: "If any man will come after me, let him deny himself, and take up his cross, and follow me." Note it well. I must deny myself and take Jesus himself as my life—I must choose. There are two lives—the self life and the Christ life; I must choose one of the two. "Follow me," says our Lord. "Make me the law of your existence, the rule of your conduct; give me your whole heart; follow me, and I will care for all." Oh, friends, it is a solemn exchange to have set before us: to come and, seeing the danger of this self with its pride and its wickedness, to cast ourselves before the Son of God, saying, "I deny my own life. I take Thy life to be mine."

The reason why Christians pray and pray for the Christ life to come into them, without result, is that the self life is not denied. You ask, "How can I get rid of this self life?" Remember the parable of the strong man who kept his house until one stronger than he came in and cast him out. Then the place was garnished and swept, but empty, and he came back with seven other spirits worse than himself. It is only Christ himself coming into our lives who can conquer the self life. Remember the apostle Paul who had seen the heavenly vision. Lest he should exalt himself, Christ sent a thorn in the flesh to humble him. There was a tendency to exalt himself, which was natural, and it would have conquered Paul, but Christ delivered him from it by His faithful care for His loving servant.

Jesus Christ is able, by His divine grace, to prevent the power of self from ever asserting itself or gaining the upper hand. Jesus Christ is willing to become the life of the soul. He is willing to teach us so to follow Him, and to have heart and life set upon Him alone, that He shall ever and always be the light of our souls. Then we can say with the apostle Paul, "Not I, but Christ liveth in me." The two truths go together. First, "not I," then, "but Christ liveth in me."

Let us look at Peter again. Christ said to him, "Deny yourself, and follow me." Whither had he to follow? Jesus led him even though he failed; and where did He lead him? He led him on to Gethsemane, and there Peter failed, for he slept when he ought to have been awake, watching and praying. He led him on towards Calvary, to the place where Peter denied Him. Was that Christ's leading? Praise God, it was. The Holy Spirit had not yet come in His power. Peter was yet a carnal man—the spirit willing, but not able to conquer; the flesh weak. What did Christ do? He led Peter on until he was broken down in utter self-abasement and humbled in the depths of sorrow. Jesus led him on, past the grave, through the resurrection, up to Pentecost. And then the Holy Spirit came, and in the Holy Spirit Christ with His divine life came. Now Peter could say, "Christ liveth in me."

There is but one way of being delivered from this life of self. We must follow Christ, set our hearts upon Him, listen to His teachings, give ourselves to Him every day that He may be all to us; and by the power of Christ the denial of self will be a blessed, unceasing reality. Never for one hour do I expect the Christian to reach a stage at which he can say, "I have no self to deny"; never for one moment in which he can say, "I do not need to deny self." No, this fellowship with the cross of Christ will be an unceasing denial of self every hour and every moment by the grace of God. We are to be crucified with Christ Jesus. We are to live with Him as those who have been baptized into His death. Think of that! Christ had no sinful self, but He had a self and that self He actually gave up unto death. In Gethsemane He said, "Father, not my will." That unsinning self He gave up unto death that He might receive it again out of the grave from God, raised up and glorified. Can we expect to go to heaven in any other way than He went? Beware! Remember that Christ descended into death and the grave, and it is in the death of self, following Jesus to the uttermost, that the deliverance and the life will come.

And now, how should we use this lesson from the Master? The first lesson will be that we should take time to humble ourselves before God at the thought of what this self is in us; acknowledge that self is the cause for every sin, every shortcoming, all failure, and all that has been dishonoring to God, and say, "Lord, this is what I am." Then let us allow Jesus Christ to take entire control of our life, in the faith that His life can be ours.

Do not think it is an easy thing to get rid of the carnal self. At a consecration meeting, it is easy to make a vow, to offer a prayer, and to perform an act of surrender, but as solemn as the death of Christ was on Calvary—His giving up of His unsinning self life to God—just as solemn must it be between us and our God—the giving up of self to death. The power of the death of Christ must come to work in us every day. Oh, think what a contrast there is between the self-willed Peter and Jesus giving up His will to God! What a contrast between the self-exaltation of Peter and the deep humility of the Lamb of God, meek and lowly in heart before God and man! What a contrast between the self-confidence of Peter and that deep dependence of Jesus upon the Father when He said, "I can do nothing of myself."

We are called upon to live the life of Christ, and Christ comes to live His life in us. But one thing must first take place: we must learn to deny and hate this self. As Peter said when he denied Christ, "I have nothing to do with him," so we must say, "I have nothing to do with self," that Christ Jesus may be all in all. Let us humble ourselves at the thought of what this self has done to us and how it has dishonored Jesus. Let us pray very fervently, "Lord, by Thy light discover this self; we beseech Thee to discover it to us. Open our eyes that we may see what it has done, and that it is the only hindrance that has been keeping us back." Let us pray that fervently, and then let us wait upon God until we get away from all our religious exercises, all our religious experience, and from all our blessings until we get close to God, with this one prayer: "Lord God, self changed an archangel into a devil, and self ruined my first parents and brought them out of Paradise into darkness and misery. Self has also been the ruin of my life and the cause of every failure; oh, discover it to me."

And then comes the blessed exchange, when a man is made willing and able to say, "Another will live the life for me, another will live with me, another will do all for me." Nothing else will do. Deny self; take up the cross to die with Jesus; follow Him only. May He give us the grace to understand, to receive, and to live the Christ life.

# 3
## Waiting on God

*Psalm 62:5—My soul, wait thou only upon God; for my expectation is from him.*

The solemn question comes to us, "Is the God I have a God that is to me above all circumstances, nearer to me than any circumstance can be?" Brother, have you learned to live your life knowing God is with you in such reality every moment that in the most difficult circumstances He is always more present and nearer than anything around you? All our knowledge of God's Word will help us very little unless that question is answered in our lives.

Why do so many of God's beloved children complain continually, "My circumstances separate me from God; my trials, my temptations, my character, my temper, my friends, my enemies, anything can come between my God and me"? Is God not able to take possession so that He can be nearer to me than anything in the world? Must riches or poverty, joy or sorrow, have a greater power over me than my God? No. But why, then, do God's children so often complain that their circumstances separate them from Him? There can be but one answer, "They do not know their God." If there is trouble or feebleness in the church of God, it is because of this. We do not know the God we have. That is why in addition to the promise, "I will be thy God," the promise is so often added, "And ye shall know that I am your God." If I know that, not through man's teaching, not with my mind or my imagination, but in the living evidence which God gives in my heart, then I know that the divine presence of my God will be so wonderful, and my God himself will be so beautiful, and so near, that I can live all my days and years a conqueror through Him that loved me. Is not that the life which we need?

The question comes again: Why is it that God's people do not know their God? And the answer is: They take anything rather than God—ministers, preaching, books, prayers, work, and efforts, any exertion of human nature, instead of waiting, and waiting long if need be, until God reveals himself. No teaching that we may get and no effort that we may put forth can put us in possession of this blessed light of God, who is all in all to our souls. But still it is attainable, it is within reach, if God will reveal himself. That is the one necessity I would to God that everyone would ask himself whether he has said, and is saying, every day, "I want more of God. Do not speak to me only of the beautiful truth there is in the Bible. That cannot satisfy me. I want God." In our inner Christian life, in our everyday prayers, in our Christian living, in our churches, in our prayer meetings, in our fellowship, it must come to that—that God always has first place; and if that be given Him, He will take possession.

Oh, if in our lives as individuals every eye were set upon the living God, every heart were crying, "My soul thirsteth for God," what power, what blessing, and what presence of the everlasting God would be revealed to us! Let me use an illustration. When a man is giving an illustrated lecture, he often uses a long pointer to indicate places on a map or chart. Do the people look at that pointer? No, that only helps to show them the place on the map. It might be of fine gold, but the *pointer* cannot satisfy them. They want to see what the pointer points at. And this Bible is nothing but a pointer, pointing to God; and—may I say it with reverence—Jesus Christ came to point us, to show us the way, to bring us to God. I am afraid there are many people who love Christ and who trust in Him, but who fail to understand the one great object of His work; they have never learned to understand what the Scripture saith, "He died, that he might bring us unto God."

There is a difference between the way and the end which I am aiming at. I might be traveling amid most beautiful scenery, in the most delightful company; but if I have a home to which I want to go, all the scenery, all the company, and all the beauty and happiness around me cannot satisfy me. I want to reach the end. I want my home. And God is meant to be the home of our souls. Christ came into the world to bring us back to God, and unless we take Christ for what God intended we should, our religion will always be a divided one. What do we read in Hebrews 7? "He is able to save to the uttermost." Whom? "Them that come to God by him"; not those who come only to Christ. In Christ—bless His name—we have the graciousness, the condescension, and the tenderness of God. But we are in danger of standing there, being content with that. Christ wants to bring us back to rejoice in the glory of God himself—in His righteousness, His holiness, His authority, His presence and His power. He can save completely those who come to God through Him!

Now, just a few thoughts on the way I can come to know God as the God above all circumstances, filling my heart and life every day. The one thing needful is: I must wait upon God. The original is, "My soul is silent into God" (Dutch version and marginal reading). What ought to be the silence of the soul unto God? A soul conscious of its littleness, its ignorance, its prejudices and its dangers from passion, from all that is human and sinful, saying, "I want the everlasting God to come in and take such hold of me that I may be kept in the hollow of His hand all my life. I want Him to take such possession of me that every moment He may work all in all in me." That is what is implied in the very nature of our God. How we ought to be silent unto Him and wait upon Him!

May I ask, with reverence, What is God for? God is for this: to be the light and the life of creation, the source and power of all existence. The beautiful trees, the green grass, the bright sun God created that they might show forth His beauty, His wisdom and His glory. Think of a tree one hundred years old. When it was planted, God did not give it a stock of life by which to carry on its existence. Nay, verily, every year God clothes the tree with its foliage and its fruit; every year He clothes the lilies afresh with their beauty. Every day and every hour it is God who maintains the life of all nature. And God created us that we might be the empty vessels in which He could work out His beauty, His will, His love, and the likeness of His blessed Son. That is what God is for, to work in us by His mighty operation without one moment's ceasing. When I begin to get hold of that, I no longer think of the true Christian life as a high impossibility and an unnatural thing, but I say, "It is the most natural thing in creation that God should have me every moment, and that my God should be nearer to me than all else." What folly it is to imagine that I cannot expect God to be with me every moment. Just look at the sunshine. Have you ever had any trouble working, studying, or reading a book in the light the sun gives? Have you ever said, "Oh, how can I keep that light? How can I hold it fast? How can I be sure that I shall continue to have it to use?" You never thought that. God has taken care that the sun itself should provide you with light, and without your care; the light comes unbidden. And I ask you: What think you? Has God arranged that the light of that sun that will one day be burned up can come to you unconsciously and abide in you blessedly and mightily; and is God not willing, or is He not able, to let His light and His presence so shine through you that you can walk all the day with God nearer to you than anything in nature?

Praise God for the assurance. He can do it. But why does He not do it more? Why so seldom and why in such feeble measure? There is but one answer: you do not let Him. You are so occupied and filled with other things, religious things, preaching and praying, studying and working, so occupied with your religion that you do not give God the time to make himself known, and to enter in and take possession. Oh, brother, listen to the word of the man who knew God so well, and begin to say, "My soul, wait thou only upon God."

I might show that this is the very glory of the Creator, the very life Christ brought into the world, the life He lived, and the very life Christ wants to lift us up to in its entire dependence on the Father. The very secret of Christ's life was this: He had such a consciousness of God's presence that whether it was Judas, who came to betray Him, or Caiaphas, who condemned Him unjustly, or Pilate, who gave Him up to be crucified, the presence of the Father was upon Him, and within Him, and around Him. Man could not touch His spirit. And that is what God wants to be to you and to me. Does not all your anxious restlessness and futile effort prove that you have not let God do His work? God is drawing you to himself. This is not your own wish, or the stirring of your own heart. It is the everlasting Divine magnet who is drawing you. These restless yearnings and thirstings, remember, are the work of God. Come and be still and wait upon God. He will reveal himself.

And how am I to wait on God? In answer I would say: First of all, in prayer take more time to be still before God without saying one word. What is the most important thing in prayer? That I catch the ear of Him to whom I speak. We are not ready to offer our petition until we are fully conscious of having secured the attention of God. You tell me you know all that. Yes, you know it; but you need to have your heart filled by the Holy Spirit with the holy consciousness that the everlasting, almighty God is indeed come very near you. The loving one is longing to have you for His own. Be still before God, and wait, and say, "O God, take possession. Reveal thyself, not to my thoughts or imaginations, but by the solemn, awe-bringing, soul-subduing consciousness that God is shining upon me, bring me to the place of dependence and humility.''

Prayer may be indeed waiting upon God, but there is a great deal of prayer that is not waiting upon God. Waiting on God is the first and the best beginning for prayer. When we bow in the humble, silent acknowledgment of God's glory and nearness before we begin to pray, there will be the very blessing that we often get only at the end. From the very beginning I come face to face with God. I am in touch with the everlasting omnipotence of love and I know my God will bless me. Let us never be afraid to be still before God. We shall then carry that stillness into our work. And when we go to church on Sunday, or to the prayer meeting on weekdays, it will be with the one desire that nothing may stand between us and God, and that we may never be so occupied with hearing and listening so that we forget the presence of God.

Oh, that God might make every minister what Moses was at the foot of Mount Sinai! ''Moses led the people out to meet God,'' and they did meet Him until they were afraid. Let every minister ask, with all the earnestness his soul can command, that God may deliver him from the sin of preaching and teaching without making the people feel first of all: "The man wants to bring us to God himself." It can be felt, not only in the words, but in the very disposition of the humble, waiting, worshiping heart. We must carry this waiting into all our worship. We will have to make a study of it; we will have to speak about it; we will have to help each other, for the truth has been too much lost in the church of Christ. We must wait upon God about it. Then we shall be able to carry it out into our daily life. There are so many Christians who wonder why they fail; but think of the ease with which they talk and join in conversation, spending hours in it, never thinking that all this may be dissipating the soul's power and leading them to spend hours not in the immediate presence of God. I am afraid this is the great difficulty: We are not willing to make the needed sacrifice for a life of continual waiting upon God. Are there not some of us who would feel it an impossibility to spend every moment under the covering of the Most High, "in the secret of his pavilion"? Beloved, do not think it too high or too difficult. It is too difficult for you and me to attain, but our God will give it to us. Let us begin even now to wait more earnestly and intensely upon God. Let us in our homes sometimes bow a little in silence. Let us in our closets wait in silence, and make a covenant, it may be, without words, that with our whole hearts we will seek God's presence to come in upon us.

What is religion? Just as much as you have of God working in you. And if you want more religion, more grace, more strength and more fruitfulness, you must have more of God. Let that be the cry of our hearts—more of God! more of God! more of God! And let us say to our souls, "My soul, wait thou upon God, for my expectation is from him."

# 4

## Entrance into Rest

*Hebrews 4:1—Let us therefore fear, lest, a promise being left us of entering into his rest, any of you should seem to come short of it.*

*Hebrews 4:11—Let us labour therefore to enter into that rest, lest any man fall after the same example of unbelief.*

I want, in the simplest way possible, to answer the question: "How does a man enter into that rest?" and to point out the simple steps that he takes—all included in the one act of surrender and faith.

The first step is this: learn to say, "I believe, heartily, there is rest in a life of faith." Israel passed through two stages. This is beautifully expressed in Deuteronomy 5: He brought us out that He might bring us in—two parts of God's work of redemption. He brought us out from Egypt that He might bring us into Canaan. And that is applicable to every believer. At your conversion, God brought you out of Egypt, and the same almighty God is longing to bring you into the Canaan life. You know how God brought the Israelites out, but they would not let Him bring them in, so they had to wander for forty years in the wilderness—the type of so many Christians. God brings them out in conversion, but they will not let Him bring them in into all that He has prepared for them. To a man who asks me, "How can I enter into the rest?" I say, first of all, speak this word, "I do believe that there is a rest into which Jesus, our Joshua, can bring a trusting soul." And if you would know the difference between the two lives— the life you have been leading and the life you now want to lead—just look at the wilderness and Canaan. In the wilderness, wandering for forty years, backward and forward; in Canaan, perfect rest in the land that God gave them. That is the difference between the life of a Christian who has, and one who has not, entered into Canaan. In the wilderness, a life of ups and downs, wandering backward and forward; going after the world and coming back and repenting; led astray by temptation and returning only to go off again. In Canaan, on the other hand, a life of rest because the soul has learned to trust: "God keeps me every hour in His mighty power."

There is a second difference: the life

in the wilderness was a life of want; in
Canaan, a life of plenty. In the wilderness
there was nothing to eat and often no water.
God graciously supplied their wants by
the manna, and the water from the rock.
But, alas! they were not content with that,
and their life was one of want and mur-
murings. But in Canaan God gave them
vineyards that they had not planted. The
old corn of the land was there waiting for
them. It was a land flowing with milk and
honey, a land that lived by the rain of heav-
en and had the very care of God himself.
Oh, Christian, come and say today, "I believe there is the possibility of such a
change out of the life of spiritual death,
and darkness, and sadness, and complain-
ing that I have often lived, into the land
where every want is supplied, where the
grace of Jesus is proved sufficient every
day, every hour. Say today, "I believe in
the possibility of such a land of rest for
me."

There is a third difference: In the wilderness there was no victory. When the Israelites tried, after they had sinned at Ka-
desh, to go up against their enemies, they
were defeated. In the land they conquered
every enemy; from Jericho onward, they
went from victory to victory. And so God
waits, Christ waits, and the Holy Spirit

waits to give victory every day—not freedom from temptation, no, not that; but in union with Christ a power that can say, "I can do all things through Christ which strengtheneth me" (Phil. 4:13). "We are more than conquerors through him that loved us" (Rom. 8:37). May God help every heart to say that.

Then comes the second step. I want you to say not only, "I believe there is such a life," but also, "I do not have it yet." Some may say, "I have sought it"; some may say, "I have never heard about it"; some may say, "At times I thought I had found it, but I lost it again." Let everyone be honest with God.

And now, you who have never yet found it begin to say, "Lord, up to this time I have never had it." Why is it of such consequence to speak thus? Because, dear friends, some people want to glide into this life of rest gradually, to steal in quietly, and God won't have it. Your life in the wilderness has been not only a life of sadness to yourself, but of sin and dishonor to God. Every deeper entrance into salvation must always be by conviction and confession; therefore, let every Christian be willing to say, "Alas! I have not lived that life, and I am guilty. I have dishonored God. I have been like Israel. I have provoked Him to wrath by my unbelief and disobedience. God have mercy upon me!" Oh, let this secret confession go up before God: "I haven't it; alas! I have not glorified God by a life in the land of rest."

Now the third step: I want you to say, "Thank God, that life is for me." Some say, "I believe there is such a life, but not for me." There are people who continually say, "Oh, my character is so unstable; my will is naturally very weak; my temperament is nervous and excitable, it is impossible for me always to live without worry, resting in God." Beloved brother, do not say that. You say so only for one reason: You do not know what your God will do for you. Do begin to look away from self and to look up to God. Take that precious word: "He brought them out that he might bring them in." The God who took them through the Red Sea was the God who took them through Jordan into Canaan. The God who converted you is the God who is able to give you this blessed life every day. Oh, begin to say, with the beginnings of a feeble faith, even before you claim it, begin even intellectually to say, "It is for me. I do believe that. God does not disinherit any of His children. What He gives is for everyone. I believe that blessed life is waiting for me. It is meant for me. God is waiting to bestow it and to work it in me. Glory be to His blessed name! My soul says it is for me, too." Oh, take that little word "me" and looking up in the very face of God dare to say, "This inestimable treasure—it is for me, the weakest and the unworthiest; it is for me." Have you said that? Say it now, "This life is possible for me, too."

The fourth step is to say: "I can never, by any effort of mine, grasp it. It is God who must bestow it on me." I want you to be very bold in saying, "It is for me." But then I want you to fall down very low and say, "I cannot seize it. I cannot take it to myself." How, then, can you get it? Praise God, if once He has brought you to a consciousness of utter helplessness and self-despair, then He can draw nigh and ask you, "Will you trust your God to work this in you?" Dearly beloved Christians, say in your heart, "I never, by any effort, can take hold of God, or seize this for myself. It is God who must give it." Cherish this blessed impotence. It is He who brought us out. It is He who must bring us in. It is your greatest happiness to be impotent. Pray God by the Holy Spirit to reveal to you this true impotence, and that will open the way for your faith to say, "Lord, Thou must do it, or it will never be done." God will do it.

People wonder, when they hear so many

sermons about faith, and such earnest pleading to believe, why it is they cannot believe. There is just one answer: self. Self is working, is trying, is struggling, and self must fail. But when you come to the end of self and can only cry, "Lord, help me! Lord, help me!" then the deliverance is nigh; believe that. It was God who brought the people in. It is God who will bring you in.

One should be willing to give up everything for the sake of this rest. The grace of God is very free. It is given without money and without price. And yet, on the other hand, Jesus said that every man who wants the pearl of great price must sacrifice his all, must sell all that he has to buy that pearl. It is not enough to see the beauty, the attractiveness and the glory, and almost taste the gladness and the joy of this wonderful life as it has been set before you. You must become the possessor, the owner of the field. The man who found the field with a treasure and the man who found the great pearl were both glad, but they did not yet possess it. They had found it, seen it, desired it, rejoiced in it; but they had not yet obtained it. It was not theirs until they sold all, gave up everything, and bought the ground and the pearl.

Ah, friends, there is a great deal that has to be given up: the world, its pleasures, its favor, its good opinion. Your relationship to the world is to be the same as Jesus' was. The world rejected Him and cast Him out, and you are to take up the position of your Lord, to whom you belong, and to follow with the rejected Christ. You have to give up everything. You have to give up all that is good in yourself and be humbled in the dust of death. And that is not all. Your past religious life and experience and successes must be given up. You must become nothing that God alone may have the glory. God has brought you out in conversion; it was God's own life given you. But you have defiled it with disobedience and unbelief. Give it all up. Give up all your own wisdom and thoughts about God's work. How hard it is for the minister of the gospel to give up all his wisdom, to lay it at the feet of Jesus and become a fool and say: "Lord, I know nothing as I should know it. I have been preaching the gospel, but how little I have seen of the glory of the blessed land and the blessed life!"

Why is it that the Holy Spirit cannot teach us more effectually? No reason but this: the wisdom of man prevents it; the wisdom of man prevents the light of God

from shining in. And so we could say of
other things: give up all. Some may have
an individual sin to give up. There may
be a Christian man who is angry with his
brother. There may be a Christian woman
who has quarreled with her neighbor. There
may be friends who are not living as they
should. There may be Christians holding
fast some little doubtful thing, not willing
to surrender and leave behind the entire
wilderness life and lust.

Oh, do take this step and say: "I am
ready to give up everything to have this
pearl of great price: my time, my attention, my business. I count all subordinate
to this rest of God as the first thing in my
life. I yield all to walk in perfect fellowship
with God." You cannot get that and live
every day in perfect fellowship with God
without giving time to it. You take time
for everything. How many hours a day has
a young lady spent for years and years that
she may become proficient on the piano?
How many years does a young man study
to fit himself for the profession of law or
medicine? Hours, days, weeks, months,
and years, gladly given up to perfect himself for his profession. And do you expect
that religion is so cheap that without giving
time you can find close fellowship with
God? You cannot. But, oh, my brothers

and sisters, the pearl of great price is worth everything. God is worth everything. Christ is worth everything.

Oh, come today and say, "Lord, at any cost help me. I do want to live this life." And if you find it difficult to say this, and if there is a struggle within the heart, never mind. Say to God, "Lord, I thought I was willing, but I see how much unwillingness there is; come and discover what the evil is still in the heart." By His grace, if you will lie at His feet and trust Him, you may be certain that deliverance will come.

Then comes the fifth step, and that is to say: "I do now give myself to the holy and everlasting God for Him to lead me into this perfect rest." Ah, friends, we must learn to meet God face to face. My sin has been against God. David felt that when he said, "Against thee, thee only, have I sinned" (Ps. 51:4).

It is God on the judgment seat whose face you will have to meet personally. It is God himself, personally, who met you to pardon your sins. Come today and put yourself into the hands of the living God. God is love. God is near. God is waiting to give you His blessing. The heart of God is waiting to give you His blessing. The heart of God is yearning over you.

"My child," God says, "you think you are longing for rest; it is I that am longing for you, because I desire to rest in your heart as My home, as My temple." You need your God. Yes, but your God needs you, to find the full satisfaction of His Father heart in Christ in you. Come today and say, "I do now give myself to Christ. I have made the choice. I deliberately say, 'Lord God, I am the purchaser of the pearl of great price. I give up everything for it. In the name of Jesus I accept that life of perfect rest.'"

And then comes my last thought. When you have said that, then add, "And now, I trust God to make it all real to me in my experience. Whether I am to live one year, or thirty years, I have heard it today again: 'God is Jehovah, the great I AM of the everlasting future, the eternal One. And thirty years hence is to Him just the same as now'; and that God gives himself to me, not according to my power to hold Him, but according to His almighty power of love to hold me."

Will you trust God today for the future? Oh, will you look up to God in Christ Jesus once again? A thousand times you have heard and thought: "God has given us His Son." But will you not today say, "How shall He not with Him give me all things,

every moment and every day of my life?"
Say that in faith. "How shall God not be
willing to keep me in the light of His coun-
tenance, in the full experience of Christ's
saving power? Did God make the sun to
shine so brightly; is the light so willing to
pour itself into every nook and corner where
it can find entrance? If so, will not my
God, who is love, be willing all the day
to shine into this heart of mine, from
morning to night, from year's end to year's
end?" God is love and longs to give himself
to us.

Oh, come, Christians, you have hitherto
lived a life in your own strength. Will you
not begin today? Will you not choose a
life in which God shall be all and in which
you rest in Him for all? Will you not choose
a life in which you shall say, "O God, I
ask, I expect, I trust Thee for it. I enter
this day into your rest, to let you keep me;
to let you keep me every hour. I enter
into the rest of God." Are you ready to
say that? Be of good courage; fear not,
you can trust God. He brings into rest. Listen to God's word in the Prophets once
again, "Take heed, and be quiet. Fear not,
neither be faint-hearted." Joshua brought
Israel into the land. God did it through
Joshua; and Joshua is Jesus, your Jesus,
who washed you in His blood; your Jesus,

whom you have learned to know as a precious Saviour. Trust Him afresh today: "O my Joshua, take me, bring me in and I will trust Thee, and in Thee the Father." You may count upon it. He will take you and the work will be done.

# 5

## The Kingdom First

*Matthew 6:33—Seek ye first the king-
dom of God.*

You have heard of the great need for
unity in Christian life and Christian work.
And where is the bond of unity between
the life of the church, the life of the individual believer and the work to be done among
the heathen? One of the expressions for
that unity is: "Seek ye first the kingdom
of God." That does not mean, as many
people take it, "Seek salvation; seek to get
into the kingdom, and then thank God and
rest there." Ah, no; the meaning of that
word is entirely different and infinitely
larger. It means: Let the Kingdom of God,
in all its breadth and length, in all its
heavenly glory and power, be the one thing
you live for, and all other things will be
added unto you. "Seek ye first the kingdom
of God."

Let me just try to answer two very
simple questions: (1) "Why should the
Kingdom of God be first?" (2) "How can

it be attained?" First, "Why should the Kingdom of God be first?" God has created us as reasonable beings, so that the more cearly we see that according to the law of nature, according to the fitness of things, if something is set before us as proper and an absolute necessity, we then are more willing to accept it and aim after it. And now, why does Christ say, "Seek ye first the kingdom of God"? If you want to understand the reason, look at God and look at man.

Look at God. Who is God? The great Being for whom alone the universe exists; in whom alone it can have its happiness. It came from Him. It cannot find any rest or joy apart from Him. Oh, that Christians understood and believed that God is a fountain of happiness—perfect, everlasting blessedness! What would the result be? Every Christian would say, "The more I can have of God, the happier I am. The more of God's will, and the more of God's love, and the more of God's fellowship, the happier I am." If Christians believed that with their whole heart, they would, with the utmost ease, give up everything that would separate them from God. Why is it that we find it so difficult to hold fellowship with God? A young minister once said to me, "Why is it that I have so much more interest in study than in prayer? How can you teach me the art of fellowship with God?" My answer was, "Oh, my brother, if we have any true conception of what God is, the art of fellowship with Him will come naturally and will be a delight."

Yes, if we believed God to be only joy to the one who comes to Him, only a fountain of unlimited blessing, how we would give up all for Him! Has not joy a far stronger attraction than anything in the world? Is it not in every beauty, or in every virtue, in every pursuit—the joy that is set before us—that draws? And if we believe that God is a fountain of joy, and sweetness, and power to bless, how our hearts will turn aside from everything and say: "Oh, the beauty of my God! I rejoice in Him alone." But alas! the Kingdom of God to many seems like a burden, something unnatural. It looks like a strain, so we seek some relaxation in the world. God is not our chief joy.

I come to you with a good message. It is right because God is infinite love, infinite blessing; it is right and more: it is our highest privilege to listen to Christ's words and to seek God and His kingdom first and above everything.

Now let us look at man, at man's

nature. What was man created for? To live in the likness of God and in His image. Now, if we have been created in the image and likeness of God, we can find our happiness in nothing except that in which God finds His happiness. The more like Him we are the happier we will be. And in what does God find His happiness? In two things: everlasting righteousness and everlasting beneficence. God is righteousness everlasting. "He is light, and in him is no darkness." The kingdom, the domination, the rule of God will bring us nothing but righteousness. "Seek ye first the kingdom of God, and his righteousness." If men but knew what sin is, and if men really longed to be free from everything like sin, what a grand message this would be! Jesus comes to lead us to God and His righteousness. We were created to be like God in His perfect righteousness and holiness. What a prospect!

We are also to be like Him in His love. The Kingdom of God means this: In God there is a rule of universal love. He loves, and loves, and never ceases to love; and He longs to bless all who will yield to His pleadings. God is light and God is love. And now the message comes to man. Can you think of a higher nobility; can you think of anything grander than to take the position that God takes, and to be one with God in His kingdom—i.e., to have His kingdom fill your heart; to have God himself as your King and portion?

Yes, my friends, let us remember that we must not just try to get the blessings of the kingdom here and there. The glory of the kingdom is this: that God is all in all. The French Empire, when Napoleon lived, had military glory as the ideal. Every Frenchman's heart thrilled at the name of Napoleon as the man who had given the empire its glory. If we realized what it means to have God bring us into His kingdom and put His kingdom into us, and with the kingdom to have God himself, that blessed One, possessing us—surely there would be nothing like this to move our hearts in enthusiasm. The Kingdom of God first! Blessed be His name!

Look at man. I don't speak about man's sins, and about man's wretchedness, and about man's seeking everywhere for pleasure, rest, and deliverance from sin, but I just say, "Think what man is by creation and then think what man is now by redemption." Let every heart say, "It is right. There is no blessedness or glory like that of the kingdom. The Kingdom of God ought to be first in my whole life and being."

But now comes the important question,

"How can I attain this?" This is the question that is troubling the lives of tens of thousands of Christians throughout the world. And it is strange that it is so very difficult for them to find the answer; that tens of thousands are not able to give an answer; and others, when the answer is given, cannot understand it. The day the centurion found his joy in being devoted to the Roman Empire, it took charge of him with all its power and glory.

Dear friends, how are we to attain to this blessed position in which the Kingdom of God shall fill our hearts with such enthusiasm that it will spontaneously be first every day? The answer first of all is, give up everything for it. You have heard of the Roman soldier who gave up his soul, his affection, his life—everything—to be a soldier. You have often read in history, both ancient and modern, how men who were not soldiers gave up their lives in sacrifice for a king or a country. You have heard how in the South African Republic not many years ago the war of liberty was fought. After three years of oppression by the English the people said they would endure it no longer, and so they gathered together to fight for their liberty. They knew how weak they were, compared with the English power, but they said, "We must

have our liberty." They bound themselves
together to fight for it, and when that vow
had been made, they went to their homes
to prepare for the struggle. Such a thrill
of enthusiasm passed through that country
that in many cases women, when their
husbands might have been allowed to stay
at home, said to them, "No, go, even though
you have not been commanded." And there
were mothers who, when one son was called
out to the front, said, "No, take two, three."
Every man and woman was ready to die.
It was in very deed "Our country first before everything."

And even so must it be with you if you
want this wonderful Kingdom of God to
take possession of you. I pray that you,
by the mercies of God, will give up everything for it. You may not know at first what
that means, but take the words and speak
them out at the footstool of God: "Anything, everything, for the Kingdom of God."
Persevere in that, and by the Holy Spirit
your God will begin to open to you the
double blessing: the blessedness of the
kingdom which comes to possess your
heart, and the blessedness of being surrendered to Him and sacrificing and giving
up all for Him.

"The Kingdom of God first!" How am
I to reach that blessed life? The answer

is: "Give up everything for it." And then a second answer would be this: Live every day and hour of your life in the humble desire to maintain that position. There are people who hear this test, who say it is true, and that they want to obey it. But if you were to ask them how much time they spend with God day by day, you would be surprised and grieved to hear how little time they give up to Him. And yet they wonder that the blessedness of the divine life disappears. We prove the value we attach to things by the time we devote to them. The kingdom should be first every day and all day. Let the kingdom be first every morning. Begin the day with God, and God himself will maintain His kingdom in your heart. Do believe that.

Rome did its utmost to maintain the authority of the man who gave himself to live for it. And God, the living God, will He not maintain His authority in your soul if you submit to Him? He will indeed. Come to Him; only come and give yourself up to Him in fellowship through Christ Jesus. Seek to maintain that fellowship with God all day. Ah, friends, a man cannot have the Kingdom of God first, and at times, by way of relaxation, throw it off and seek his enjoyment in the things of this world. People have a secret idea that life will become too solemn, too great a strain; it will be too difficult every moment of the day, from morning to evening, to have the Kingdom of God first. One sees at once how wrong it is to think thus. The presence of the love of God must every moment be our highest joy. Let us say, "By the help of God, it shall ever be the Kingdom of God first."

My final answer to that question, "How can it be?" is that it can be only by the power of the Holy Ghost. Let us remember that God's Word exhorts us to "be filled with the Spirit." And if you are content with less of the Spirit than God offers, not utterly and entirely yielding to be filled with the Spirit, you are not obeying the command. But listen: God has made a wonderful provision. Jesus Christ came preaching the gospel of the kingdom and proclaimed, "The kingdom is at hand." "Some," He said, "are standing here who will not see death until they see the kingdom come in power." He said to the disciples, "The kingdom is within you." And when did the kingdom come, that Kingdom of God upon earth? When the Holy Ghost descended. On Ascension Day the King went and sat down upon the throne at the right hand of God, and the Kingdom of God, in Christ, the Kingdom of Heaven upon earth, was inaugurated.

When the Holy Ghost came down He

brought God and Christ into the heart and
established the rule of God in power. I
am afraid sometimes that in speaking of
the Holy Spirit we forget one thing. The
Holy Spirit is very much spoken of in connection with power; and it is right that we
should seek power. But He is not mentioned
much in connection with the graces. And
yet these are always more important than
the gifts of power. Holiness, humility,
meekness, gentleness, and lovingness—
these are the true marks of the kingdom.
We speak rightly of the Holy Spirit as the
only one who can breathe all this into us.
But I think there is a third thing almost
more important, and that is: In the Spirit,
the Father and the Son themselves come.
When Christ first promised the Holy Spirit
and spoke about His approaching coming,
He said, "At that day ye shall know that
I am in the Father, and ye in me, and I
in you. He that hath my commandments,
and keepeth them, he it is that loveth me:
and he that loveth me shall be loved of
my Father . . . my Father will love him,
and we will come unto him, and make our
abode with him" (John 14:20, 21, 23).
Brother, if you would have the Kingdom
of God first in your life, you must have
the kingdom in your heart. My heart may
be set upon a thing that binds me with

chains, but the moment the chains are loosened I fly towards the object of my affection and desire. Just so the kingdom must be within us, and then it is easy to say, "The kingdom first." But to have the kingdom within us in truth, we must have God the Father and Christ the Son, by the Holy Ghost within us, too. There is no kingdom without the King.

You are called to likeness with Christ. Oh, how many Christians strive after this part and that part of the likeness of Christ, and forget the root of the whole! What is the root of all? That Christ gave himself utterly to God, to His kingdom and glory. He gave His life that God's kingdom might be established. If you give your life to God to be every moment a living sacrifice, the kingdom will come with power into your heart. Give yourself to Christ. Let Christ the King reign in your heart, and the heavenly kingdom will come, and His presence and rule will be known in power. Oh, think of that wonderful event in eternity recorded in First Corinthians: God has entrusted Christ with the kingdom, but there is coming a day when Christ himself shall come again to be subjected unto the Father, and He shall give up the kingdom to the Father that God may be all. In that day Christ shall say before the universe,

"This is my glory. I give back the kingdom to the Father!"

Christians, if your Christ finds His glory here on earth in dying and sacrificing himself for the kingdom and then in eternity again in giving the kingdom to God, shall not you and I come to God to do the same and count anything we have as loss that the Kingdom of God may be made manifest and that God may be glorified?

# 7

## Christ Our Life

*Colossians 3:4—Christ, who is our life.*

One question that rises in every mind is this: "How can I live a life of perfect trust in God?" Many do not know the right answer, or the full answer. It is this: "Christ must live it in me." That is what He became man for, to live a life of trust in God and so to show us how we ought to live. When He had done that upon earth, He went to heaven that He might do more than show us, that He might give us and live in us that life of trust. It is as we understand what the life of Christ is and how it becomes ours that we shall be prepared to desire and to ask of Him that He himself would live it in us. When first we have seen what the life is, then we shall understand how it is that He can actually take possession and make us like himself.

I want especially to direct attention to that first question. I wish to set before you the life of Christ as He lived it that we may understand what He has for us and

what we can expect from Him. Christ
Jesus lived a life upon earth that He expects
us literally to imitate. We often say that
we long to be like Christ. We study the
traits of His character, mark His footsteps,
and pray for grace to be like Him, and
yet somehow we succeed but very little.
Why? Because we want to pluck the fruit
while the root is absent. If we really want
to understand what the imitation of Christ
means, we must go to that which consti-
tuted the very root of His life before God.
It was a life of absolute dependence, absolute trust, absolute surrender; and until
we are one with Him in what is the principle
of His life, it is vain to seek here or there
to copy the graces of that life.

In the Gospel story we find five great
points of special importance: Christ's birth,
His life on earth, His death, His resurrection, and His ascension. In these we have
what an old writer has called "the process
of Jesus Christ," the process by which He
became what He is today—our glorified
King and our life. In all this life process
we must be made like unto Him. Look at
the first. What have we to say about His
birth? This: He received His life *from
God.* What about His life upon earth? He
lived that life in dependence *upon God.* His
death? He gave up His life *to God.* His

resurrection? He was raised from the dead *by God*. His ascension? He lives His life in glory *with God*.

First, His birth. He received His life from God. Why is it necessary to consider that? Because that was the starting point of His whole life. He said, "The Father sent me"; "The Father hath given the Son all things"; "The Father hath given the Son to have life in himself." Christ received it as His own life, just as God has His life in himself. And yet, all the time it was a life given and received. "Because the Father almighty has given this life unto Me, the Son of man on earth, I can count upon God to maintain it and to carry me through all." And that is the first lesson we need. We need to meditate often on it, and to pray, and to think, and to wait before God until our hearts open to the wonderful consciousness that the everlasting God has a divine life within us which cannot exist but through Him.

I believe God has given His life; it roots in Him, and it must be maintained by Him. We often think that God has given us a life, a spiritual life, which is now our own, and that we are to take charge; and then we complain that we cannot keep it right. No wonder. We must learn to live as Jesus did.

I have a God-given treasure in this earthen vessel. I have the light of the knowledge of the glory of God in the face of Christ. I have the life of God's Son within me given me by God himself, and it can be maintained only by God himself as I live in fellowship with Him.

In Romans the apostle Paul teaches us that we must reckon ourselves dead unto sin but alive unto God through Christ Jesus. He goes on to say, "Therefore . . . yield yourselves [present yourselves] unto God, as those that are alive from the dead." How often a Christian hears solemn words about his being alive to God, and his having to reckon himself dead indeed to sin but alive to God in Christ! He does not know what to do. He immediately wonders, "How can I keep this death and this life?" Listen to what Paul says. The moment that you reckon yourself dead to sin and alive to God, go with that life to God himself, and present yourself as alive from the dead, and say to God, "Lord, Thou hast given me this life. Thou alone canst keep it. I bring it to Thee. I cannot understand all. I hardly know what I have but I come to Thee to perfect what Thou hast begun." To live like Christ I must be conscious every moment that my life has come from God, and He alone can maintain it.

Then, secondly, His life on earth. How did Christ live out His life during the thirty-three years in which He walked here upon earth? He lived it in dependence on God. You know how continually He says: "The Son can do nothing of himself. The words that I speak, I speak not of myself." He waited unceasingly for the teaching, and the commands, and the guidance of the Father. He prayed for power from the Father. Whatever He did, He did in the name of the Father. He, the Son of God, felt the need of much prayer, of persevering prayer, of bringing down from heaven and maintaining the life of fellowship with God in prayer. We hear a great deal about trusting God. Most blessed! And we may say, "Ah, that is what I want," but we may forget what is the very secret of all—that God, in Christ, must work all in us. I not only need God as an object of trust, but I must have Christ within as the power to trust. He must live His own life of trust in me.

Look at it in that wonderful story of Paul, the apostle, the beloved servant of God. He was in danger of self-confidence, and God in heaven sent that terrible trial in Asia to bring him down, lest he should trust in himself and not in the living God. God watched over His servant that he might

be kept trusting. Again in 2 Corinthians
12 we have the story about the thorn in the
flesh. Paul was in danger of exalting himself, and the blessed Master came to humble him and to teach him, "I keep thee
weak, that thou mayest learn to trust not
in thyself but in Me." If we are to enter into
the rest of faith, and to abide there; if we
are to live the life of victory in the land of
Canaan, it must begin here. We must be
broken down from all self-confidence and
learn like Christ to depend absolutely and
unceasingly upon God.

There is a greater work to be done in
that than we perhaps know. We must be
broken down, and the habit of our souls
must be unceasingly: "I am nothing; God
is all. I cannot walk before God as I
should for one hour unless God keep the
life He has given me." What a blessed solution God gives, then, to all our questions
and our difficulties when He says, "My
child, Christ has gone through it all for
thee. Christ hath wrought out a new nature
that can trust Me; and Christ the living
One in heaven will live in thee and enable
thee to live that life of trust." That is
why Paul said, "Such confidence have we
toward God, through Christ." What does
that mean? Does it only mean through
Christ 'as the mediator, or intercessor? Of

course not. It means much more: through Christ living in and enabling us to trust God as He trusted Him.

Third, Christ's death. What does Christ's death teach us of His relation to the Father? It opens up to us one of the deepest and most solemn lessons of the Christ life, one which the church of Christ understands all too little. We know what the death of Christ means as an atonement, and we never can emphasize too much the blessed substitution and blood-shedding by which redemption was won for us. But let us remember, that is only half the meaning of His death. The other half is this: just as much as Christ was my substitute, who died for me, just so much is He my head, in whom, and with whom, I die; and just as He lives for me to intercede, He lives in me to carry out and to perfect His life. And if I want to know what that life is which He will live in me, I must look at His death. By His death He proved that He possessed life only to hold it and to spend it for God. To the very uttermost, without the shadow of a moment's exception, He lived for God—every moment, everywhere.

Therefore, if one wants to live a life of perfect trust, there must be the perfect surrender of his life and will even unto the very death. He must be willing to go all lengths with Jesus, even to Calvary. When Jesus was twelve years of age He said, "Wist ye not that I must be about my Father's business?" and again when He came to Jordan to be baptized, "It becometh us to fulfill all righteousness." So on through all His life, He ever said, "It is my meat and drink to do the will of my Father. I came not to do my own will, but the will of him that sent me." "Lo, I am come to do thy will, O God." And in the agony of Gethsemane, His words were: "Not my will, but thine, be done."

Someone may say, "I do indeed desire to live the life of perfect trust; I desire to let Christ live it in me; I am longing to come to such an apprehension of Christ as shall give me the certainty that Christ will forever abide in me; I want to come to the full assurance that Christ, my Joshua, will keep me in the land of victory." What is needful for that? My answer is: "Take care that you do not take a false Christ, an imaginary Christ, a half Christ." And what is the full Christ? The full Christ is the man who said, "I give up everything to the death that God may be glorified. I have not a thought; I have not a wish; I would not live a moment except for the glory of God."

You say at once, "What Christian can ever attain that?" Do not ask that question; rather ask, "Has Christ attained it and does Christ promise to live in me?" Accept Him in His fullness and leave Him to teach you how far He can bring you and what He can work in you. Make no conditions or stipulations about failure, but cast yourself upon, abandon yourself to, this Christ who lived that life of utter surrender to God that He might prepare a new nature which He could impart to you and in which He might make you like himself. Then you will be in the path by which He can lead you on to blessed experience and possession of what He can do for you.

Christ Jesus came into the world with a commandment from the Father that He should lay down His life. He lived with that one thought in His bosom His whole life long. And the one thought that ought to be in the heart of every believer is this: "I am in the death with Christ—absolutely, unchangeably given up to wait upon God that God may work out His purpose and glory in me from moment to moment." Few attain the victory and the enjoyment and the full experience at once. But this you can do: Take the right attitude and as you look to Jesus and what He was, say, "Father, Thou hast made me a partaker

of the divine nature, a partaker of Christ.
It is in the life of Christ given up to Thee
to the death, in His power and indwelling,
in His likeness, that I desire to live out
my life before Thee."

Death is a solemn thing, an awful thing.
In the Garden it cost Christ great agony
to die that death. No wonder it is not easy
for us. But we willingly consent when we
have learned the secret: in death alone the
life of God will come; in death there is
blessedness unspeakable. It was this which
made Paul so willing to bear the sentence
of death in himself; he knew the God who
quickeneth the dead. The sentence of
death is on everything that is of nature.
Are we willing to accept it, do we cherish
it? Are we not rather trying to escape the
sentence or to forget it? We do not believe
fully that the sentence of death is on us,
but, again, whatever is of nature must die.
Ask God to make you willing to believe
with your heart that to die with Christ is
the only way to live in Him.

You ask, "But must it then be dying
every day?" Yes, beloved. Jesus lived every day in the prospect of the cross, and
we, in the power of His victorious life, being
made conformable to His death, must rejoice every day in going down with Him
into death. Let me illustrate. Take an oak

of some hundred years' growth. How was that oak born? In a grave. The acorn was planted in the ground, a grave was made for it that the acorn might die. It died and disappeared; it cast roots downward, and it casts shoots upward, and now that tree has been standing a hundred years. Where is it standing? In its grave; all the time in the very grave where the acorn died; it has stood there stretching its roots deeper and deeper into that earth in which its grave was made, and yet, all the time, though it stood in the very grave where it had died, it has been growing higher, and stronger, and broader, and more beautiful. And all the fruit it ever bore, and all the foliage that adorned it year by year, it owed to that grave in which its roots are cast and kept. Even so Christ owes everything to His death and His grave. And we, too, owe everything to that grave of Jesus.

Oh! let us live every day rooted in the death of Jesus. Be not afraid, but say, "To my own will I will die; to human wisdom, and human strength, and to the world I will die; for it is in the grave of my Lord that His life has its beginning, and its strength and its glory."

This brings us to our next thought. First, Christ received life from the Father; sec-

ond, Christ lived it in dependence on the
Father; third, Christ gave it up in death
to the Father; and now, fourth, Christ
received it again raised by the Father, by
the power of the glory of the Father. Oh,
the deep meaning of the resurrection of
Christ! What did Christ do when He died?
He went down into the darkness and absolute helplessness of death. He gave up
a life that was without sin; a life that was
God-given; a life that was beautiful and
precious; and He said, "I will give it into
the hands of my Father if He asks it." And
He did. He was there in the grave waiting
on God to do His will; and because He honored God to the uttermost in His helplessness, God lifted Him up to the very
uttermost of glory and power. Christ lost
nothing by giving up His life in death to
the Father.

And so, if you want the glory and the
life of God to come upon you, it is in the
grave of utter helplessness that that life
of glory will be born. Jesus was raised from
the dead, and that resurrection power, by
the grace of God, can and will work in us.
Let no one expect to live a right life until
he lives a full resurrection life in the power
of Jesus. Let me state in a different way
what this resurrection means.

Christ had a perfect life, given by God.

The Father said: "Will you give up that life to me? Will you part with it at my command?" And He parted with it, but God gave it back to Him in a second life ten thousand times more glorious than that earthly life. So God will do to every one of us who willingly consents to part with his life. Have you ever understood it? Jesus was born twice. The first time He was born in Bethlehem. That was a birth into a life of weakness. But the second time, He was born from the grave: He is the "first-born from the dead." Because He gave up the life that He had by His first birth, God gave Him the life of the second birth, in the glory of heaven and the throne of God.

Christians, that is exactly what we need to do. A man may be an earnest Christian, a successful worker. He may be a Christian who has had a measure of growth and advance; but if he has not entered this fullness of blessing, then he needs to come to a second and deeper experience of God's saving power: he needs, just as God brought him out of Egypt, through the Red Sea, to come to a point where God brings him through Jordan into Canaan. Beloved, we have been baptized into the death of Christ. It is as we say, "I have had a very blessed life. I have had many blessed experiences, and God has done many things for me; but I

am conscious there is something wrong
still. I am conscious that this life of
rest and victory is not really mine." Before
Christ got His life of rest and victory on
the throne, He had to die and give up all.
You do it, too, and you shall with Him share
His victory and glory. It is as we follow
Jesus in His death that resurrection, power,
and joy will be ours.

Then comes our last point. The fifth step
in His wondrous path—His ascension. He
was lifted up to be forever with the Father.
Because He humbled himself, therefore
God highly exalted Him. Wherein cometh
the beauty and the blessedness of that exaltation of Jesus? For himself, perfect fellowship with the Father; for others, participa-
tion in the power of God's omnipotence.
Yes, that was the fruit of His death. Scripture promises not only that God will, in
the resurrection life, give us joy, and peace
that passeth all understanding, victory over
sin, and rest in God, but He will also bap-
tize us with the Holy Ghost; or, in other
words, will fill us with the Holy Ghost. Jesus was lifted to the throne of heaven that
He might there receive from the Father the
Spirit in His new, divine manifestation, to
be poured out in His fullness.

And as we come to the resurrection life,
the life in the faith of Him who is one with

us and sits upon the throne—we too may
be partakers of the fellowship with Christ
Jesus as He ever dwells in God's presence,
and the Holy Spirit will fill us, to work in
us, and out of us, in a way that we have
never yet known.

Jesus received this divine life by depending absolutely upon the Father all His
life long, depending upon Him even down
into death. He got that life in the full glory
of the Spirit to be poured out by giving
himself up in obedience and surrender to
God alone, and even in the grave leaving
God to work out His mighty power. And that
very Christ will live out His life in you and
me. Oh, the mystery! Oh, the glory! And
oh, the divine certainty. Jesus Christ means
to live out that life in you and me. Then,
ought we not to humble ourselves before
God? Have we been Christians so many
years and realized so little what we are?
I am a vessel set apart—cleansed, emptied,
consecrated; just standing, waiting every
moment for God, in Christ, by the Holy
Spirit, to work out in me as much of the
holiness and the life of His Son as pleases
Him. And until the Church of Christ comes
to go down into the grave of humiliation,
and confession, and shame; until the church
of Christ comes to lay itself in the very
dust before God, and to wait upon Him to

do something new, something wonderful, something supernatural in lifting it up, it will remain feeble in all its efforts to overcome the world.

Within the church what lukewarmness, what worldliness, what disobedience, what sin! How can we ever fight this battle, or meet these difficulties? The answer is: Christ, the risen One, the crowned One, the almighty One, must come and live in the individual members. But we cannot expect this unless we die with Him. I referred to the tree grown so high and beautiful, yet every day for a hundred years its roots have been growing deeper in the grave in which the acorn died.

Children of God, we must go down deeper into the grave of Jesus. We must cultivate the sense of impotence, and dependence, and nothingness until our souls walk before God every day in a deep and holy trembling. God keep us from being anything. God teach us to wait on Him that He may work in us all He wrought in His Son till Christ Jesus may live out His life in us! For this may God help us!

## Christ's Humility Our Salvation

*Philippians 2:5-8—Let this mind be in you, which was also in Christ Jesus . . . he humbled himself, and became obedient unto death, even the death of the cross.*

All are familiar with this wonderful passage. Paul is speaking about one of the most simple, practical things in daily life—humility. And in connection with that, he gives us a wonderful exhibition of divine truth. In this chapter we have the eternal Godhead of Jesus—He was in the form of God and one with God. We have His incarnation—He came down and was found in the likeness of man. We have His death with the atonement—He became obedient unto death. We have his exaltation—God hath highly exalted Him. We have the glory of His kingdom—that every knee shall bow, and every tongue confess Him. And in what connection? Is it a theological study? No. Is it a description of what Christ is? No. It is in connection with a simple, downright call to a life of humility in our association with each other. Our life on earth is linked to all the eternal glory of the Godhead as revealed in the exaltation of Jesus. The very looking to Jesus, the very bowing of the knee to Jesus, ought to be inseparably connected with a spirit of the very deepest humility. Consider the humility of Jesus. First of all, that humility is our salvation; then, that humility is just the salvation we need; and again, that humility is the salvation which the Holy Spirit will give us.

Humility is the salvation that Christ brings. That is our first thought. We often have very vague—I might also say visionary—ideas of what Christ is; we love the person of Christ, but that which makes up Christ, which actually constitutes Him the Christ, we do not know or love. If we love Christ above everything, we must love humility above everything, for humility is the very essence of His life and glory, and the salvation He brings. Just think of it. Where did it begin? Is there humility in heaven? You know there is, for they cast their crowns before the throne of God and the Lamb. But is there humility on the throne of God? Yes. What was it but heavenly humility that made Jesus on the throne willing to say, "I will go down to be a servant, and to die for man; I will go and live as the meek and lowly Lamb of God"? Jesus

brought humility from heaven to us. It was
humility that brought Him to earth, or He
never would have come. In accordance with
this, just as Christ became a man in this
divine humility, so His whole life was
marked by it. He might have chosen another form in which to appear; He might have
come in the form of a king, but He chose
the form of a servant. He made himself
of no reputation; He emptied himself; He
chose the form of a servant. He said, "The
Son of Man is not come to be ministered
unto, to be served, but to serve, and to give
His life a ransom for many." And you know,
in the last night, He took the place of a
slave, girded himself with a towel, and went
to wash the feet of Peter and the other disciples. Beloved, the life of Jesus upon earth
was a life of the deepest humility. It was
this which gave His life its worth and beauty
in God's sight.

And then His death—possibly you
haven't thought of it much in this connection, but His death was an exhibition
of unparalleled humility. "He humbled himself, and became obedient unto death, even
the death of the cross." My Lord Christ
took a low place all the time He walked
upon earth. He took a very low place when
He began to wash the disciples' feet; but
when He went to Calvary, He took the low-

est place to be found in the universe of God, the very lowest, and He let sin, and the curse of sin, and the wrath of God, cover Him. He took the place of a guilty sinner that He might bear our load, that He might serve us in saving us from our wretchedness, that He might by His precious blood win deliverance for us, that He might by that blood wash us from our stain and our guilt.

We are in danger of thinking about Christ as God, as man, as the atonement, as the Saviour, and as exalted upon the throne, and we form an image of Christ, while the real Christ, that which is the very heart of His character, remains unknown. What is the real Christ? Divine humility, bowed down into the very depths for our salvation. The humility of Jesus is our salvation. We read, "He humbled himself, therefore God hath highly exalted him." The secret of His exaltation to the throne is this: He humbled himself before God and man. Humility is the Christ of God, and now in heaven, today, that Christ, the Man of humility, is on the throne of God.

What do I see? A Lamb standing, as it had been slain, on the throne; in the glory He is still the meek and gentle Lamb of God. His humility is the badge He wears there. You often use that name—the Lamb of God—and you use it in connection with the blood of the sacrifice. You sing the praise of the Lamb, and you put your trust in the blood of the Lamb. Praise God for the blood. You never can trust that too much. But I am afraid you forget that the word "Lamb" must mean to us two things: (1) a sacrifice, the shedding of blood; (2) the meekness of God, incarnate upon earth, the meekness of God represented in the meekness and gentleness of a little Lamb.

But the salvation that Christ brought is not only a salvation that flows *out* of humility; it also leads *to* humility. We must understand that this is not only the salvation which you and I need. What is the cause of all man's wretchedness? Primarily pride, man seeking his own will and his own glory. Yes, pride is the root of every sin, and so the Lamb of God comes to us in our pride and brings us salvation from it. We need above everything to be saved from our pride and our self-will. It is good to be saved from the sins of stealing, murdering, and every other evil; but a man needs above all to be saved from what is the root of all sin—his self-will and his pride. It is not until man begins to feel that this is exactly the salvation he needs that he really can understand what Christ is, and that he can accept Him as his salvation.

That is the salvation that we as Christians and believers especially need. We know the sad story of Peter and John: what their self-will and pride brought upon them. They needed to be saved from nothing except themselves, and that is the lesson which we must learn if we are to enter the life of rest.

How can we enter that life and dwell there in the bosom of the Lamb of God if pride rules? Have we not often heard complaints of how much pride there is in the church of Christ? What is the cause of all the division, strife, and envying that is often found even among God's saints? Why is it that often in a family there is bitterness—it may be only for half an hour, or half a day—hard judgments and hasty words? What is the cause of estrangement between friends? What is the cause of evil speaking? What is the cause of selfishness and indifference to the feelings of others? Simply this: the pride of man. He lifts himself up, and he claims the right to have his opinions and judgments as he pleases. The salvation we need is indeed humility, because it is only through humility that we can be restored to our right relation to God.

"Waiting upon God"—that is the only true expression for the real relation of the creature to God; to be nothing before God.

What is the essential idea of a creature made by God? It is this: to be a vessel in which He can pour out His fullness, in which He can exhibit His life, His goodness, His power, and His love. A vessel must be empty if it is to be filled, and if we are to be filled with the life of God, we must be utterly empty of self. This is the glory of God: that He is to fill all things, and especially His redeemed people. And as this is the glory of the creature, so it is the only redemption and the only glory of every redeemed soul—to be empty and as nothing before God; to wait upon Him and to let Him be all in all.

Humility has a prominent place in almost every epistle of the New Testament. Paul says, "Walk with all lowliness and meekness, with longsuffering, forbearing one another in love; endeavoring to keep the unity of the Spirit in the bond of peace." The nearer you get to God, and the fuller of God, the lowlier you will be; and equally before God and man, you will love to bow very low. We know of Peter's early self-confidence; but in his epistles what a different language he speaks! He wrote there, "Ye younger, submit yourselves unto the elder. Yea, all of you be subject one to another, humble yourselves therefore under the mighty hand of God, that he may exalt you in due time" (1 Pet. 5:5, 6). He understood, and he dared to preach, humility to all. It is indeed the salvation we need.

What is it that prevents people from coming to that entire surrender? Simply that they dare not abandon themselves and trust themselves to God. They are not willing to be nothing, to give up their wishes, and their will, and their honor to Christ. Shall we not accept the salvation that Jesus offers? He gave up His own will. He gave up His own honor. He gave up any confidence in himself and lived dependent upon God as a servant whom the Father had sent. There is the salvation we need, the Spirit of humility that was in Christ.

What is it that often disturbs our hearts and our peace? It is pride seeking to be something. And God's decree is irreversible: "God resisteth the proud, and giveth grace to the humble." How often Jesus had to speak to His disciples about it! You will find repeatedly in the Gospel those simple words: "He that humbleth himself shall be exalted; he that exalteth himself shall be humbled." He taught His desciples: "He that would be chiefest among you, let him be the servant of all." This should be our one cry before God: "Let the power of the Holy Ghost come upon me, with the humility of Jesus, that I may take the place that He took." Brother, do you want a better place than Jesus had? Are you seeking a higher place than Jesus? Or will you say, "Down, down, as deep as ever I can go. By the help of God I will be nothing before God; I will be where Jesus was."

And now comes the third thought. This is the salvation the Holy Ghost brings. You know what a change took place in those disciples. Let us praise God for it. The Holy Spirit means this: the life, the disposition, the temper, and the inclinations of Jesus brought down from heaven into our hearts. That is the Holy Ghost. He has His mighty workings to bestow as gifts; but the fullness of the Holy Ghost is this: Jesus Christ in His humility coming to dwell in us. When Christ was teaching His disciples, all His instructions may have helped in the way of preparation, breaking them down, and making them conscious of what was wrong, and awakening desire; but the instruction could not do it, and all their love to Jesus and their desire to please Him could not do it until the Holy Ghost came. That is the promise Christ gave. He says, in connection with the coming of the Holy Ghost, "I will come again to you." Christ said to His disciples, "I have been three years with you, and you have been in the closest contact with Me. I have done the utmost to reach your hearts. I have sought to get into your hearts, yet I have failed; but fear not, I will come again. In that day ye shall see Me, and your hearts shall rejoice, and no man shall take your joy from you. I will come again to dwell in you, and live My life in you."

Christ went to heaven that He might get a power which He never had before. And what was that? The power of living in men. God be praised for this! It was because Jesus, the humble One, the Lamb of God, the meek, the lowly and gentle One, came down in the Holy Spirit into the hearts of His disciples that the pride was expelled, and that the very breath of heaven breathed through Him in the love that made them one heart and one soul.

Dear friends, Christ is yours. Christ as He comes in the power of the Holy Spirit is yours. Are you longing to have Him, to have the perfect Christ Jesus? Come, then, and see how, amid the glories of His Godhead—His having been obedient to death; and amid the glories of His exaltation, which is the chief and brightest glory, He humbled himself from heaven down to earth and on earth down to the cross. He humbled himself to bear the name and show the meekness, and die the death of the Lamb of God.

And what is it we now need to do? How are we to be saved by this humility of Jesus? It is a solemn question, but, thank God, the answer can be given. First we must desire it above everything. Let us learn to pray God to deliver us from every vestige of pride, for this is a cursed thing. Let us learn to set aside for a time other things in the Christian life, and begin to plead with the Lamb of God day by day, "O Lamb of God, I know Thy love, but I know so little of Thy meekness." Come day after day and lay your heart against His heart and say to Him with strong desire, "Jesus, Lamb of God, give, oh, give me thyself, with Thy meekness and humility," and He will fulfill the desire of them that fear Him. It is not enough to desire it and to pray for it. You must claim and accept it as yours.

This humility is given you in Christ Jesus, who is our life. What does that mean? Oh, that God might give you and me a vision of what that means! The air is our life, and the air is everywhere, universal. We breathe without difficulty because God surrounds us with the air; and is the air nearer to me than Christ is? The sun gives light to every green leaf and every blade of grass, shining hour by hour and moment by moment. And is the sun nearer to the blade of grass than Christ is to man's soul?

Verily, no. Christ is around us on every
side; Christ is pressing on us to enter, and
there is nothing in heaven, or earth, or hell
that can keep the light of Christ from shining into the heart that is empty and open.
If the windows of your room were closed
with shutters, the light could not enter. It
would be on the outside of the building,
streaming and streaming against the shutters; but it could not enter. But leave the
windows without shutters, and the light
comes, it rejoices to come in and fill the
room. Even so, children of God, Jesus and
His light, Jesus and His humility, are
around you on every side, longing to enter
into your hearts. Come and take Him today
in His blessed meekness and gentleness.
Do not be afraid of Him. He is the Lamb
of God. He is so patient with you, He is
so kindly towards you, He is so tender and
loving. Take courage today and trust Jesus
to come into your heart and take possession
of it.

And when He has taken possession, there
will be a life day by day of blessed fellowship with Him, and you will feel a necessity
ever deeper for your quiet time with Him,
and for worshiping and adoring Him, and
for just sinking down before Him in helplessness and humility, and saying, "Jesus,
I am nothing, and Thou art all." It will

be a blessed life, because you will be conscious of being at the feet of Jesus. At this moment you can claim Jesus in His divine humility as the life of your soul. Will you? Will you not open your heart, and say, "Come in; come in"?

Come today and take Him afresh in this blessed power of His wonderful humility, and say to Him, "O Thou who didst say, 'Learn of me, for I am meek and lowly in heart, and ye shall find rest unto your souls,' my Lord, I know why it is that I have not the perfect life. It is my pride, but today, come Thou and dwell in my heart. Thou who didst lead even Peter and John into the blessedness of Thy heavenly humility; Thou wilt not refuse me. Lord, here I am; do Thou, who by Thy wonderful humility alone canst save, come in. O Lamb of God, I believe in Thee; take possession of my heart and dwell in me." When you have said that, go out in quiet, and retire, walking gently as holding the Lamb of God in your heart, and say, "I have received the Lamb of God. He makes my heart His care; He breathes His humility and dependence on God in me, and so brings me to God. His humility is my life and salvation."

## 8

## The Complete Surrender

*Genesis 39:1-3—Joseph was brought down to Egypt; and Potiphar, an officer of Pharaoh, captain of the guard, an Egyptian, bought him of the hands of the Ishmaelites, which had brought him down thither. And the Lord was with Joseph, and he was a prosperous man; and he was in the house of his master the Egyptian. And his master saw that the Lord was with him.*

We have in this passage an object lesson which teaches us what Christ is to us. Note: Joseph was a slave, but God was with him so distinctly that his master could see it. "And his master saw that the Lord was with him, and that the Lord made all that he did to prosper in his hands. And Joseph found grace in his sight, and he served him" —that is to say, he was his slave about his person—"and he made him overseer over his house"—that was something new. Joseph had been a slave, but now he becomes a master. "And he made him overseer over his house, and over all that he had he put into his hands. And it came to pass from the time that he had made him overseer in his house, and over all that he had, that the Lord blessed the Egyptian's house for Joseph's sake; and the blessing of the Lord was upon all that he had in the house, and in the field. And he left all that he had in Joseph's hand; and he knew not aught he had, save the bread which he did eat."

We find Joseph in two characters in the house of Potiphar: First as a servant and a slave, one who is trusted and loved, but still entirely a servant; second, as master. Potiphar made him overseer over his house and his lands and all that he had, so that we read afterward that he left everything in his hands, and he knew of nothing except the bread that came upon his table.

I want to call your attention to Joseph as a type of Christ. In the Christian life we sometimes speak of entire surrender, and rightly. Here we have a beautiful illustration of what it is. First, Joseph was in Potiphar's house to serve him and to help him. He did that, and Potiphar learned to trust him, so that he said, "All that I have I will give into his hands." Now, that is exactly what is to take place with a great many Christians. They know Christ, they trust Him, they love Him, but He is not Master. He is a sort of helper. When there is trouble they come to Him, when they sin they ask Him for pardon in His precious blood, when they are in darkness they cry to Him; but often they live according to their own will, and they seek help from themselves. But how blessed is the man who comes and, like Potiphar, says, "I will give up everything to Jesus!" There are many who have accepted Christ as their Lord, but have never yet come to the final, absolute surrender of everything.

Christians, if you want perfect rest, abiding joy, strength to work for God, oh, come and learn from that poor heathen Egyptian what you ought to do. He saw that God was with Joseph and he said, "I will give up my house to him." Oh, learn to do that. There are some who have never yet accepted Christ, some who are seeking after Him, thirsting and hungering, but they do not know how to find Him.

Let me direct your attention to four thoughts regarding this surrender to Christ: First, its motives; second, its measures; third, its blessedness; lastly, its duration.

First of all, its motives. What moved Potiphar to do this? I think the answer is very easy: he was a trusted servant of the king and he had the king's work to take care of, but he very likely could not take care of his own house. All his time and attention were required at the court of Pharaoh. He had his duty there; he was in high honor; but his own house was neglected. Very likely he had had other overseers, one slave appointed to rule the others, and perhaps that one had been unfaithful, or dishonest, and somehow his house was not as he would have it. So he bought another slave, just as he had formerly done, but in this case he saw what he had never seen before. There was something unusual about the man. He walked so humbly, he served so faithfully and so lovingly, and withal so successfully. Potiphar began to look into the reason for this, and finally concluded that God was with Joseph.

It is a grand thing to have a man with whom God is, to entrust one's business to. The heathen realized this, and between the need of his own house and what he saw in Joseph, Potiphar decided to make him overseer.

I ask you, do not these two motives plead most urgently that you should say, "I will make Jesus master over my whole being"? Your house, Christian, your spiritual life, the dwelling, the temple of God in your heart—in what state is that? Is it not often like the temple of old, in Jerusalem, that had been defiled and made a house of merchandise and afterwards a den of thieves? Your heart, meant to be the home of Jesus, is it not often full of sin and darkness, full of sadness, full of vexation? You have done your very best to get it changed, and you have called in the help of man and the help of means. You have used every method you could think of for getting it put right; but it will not come right until He whose it is comes in to take charge.

If there is any trouble in your heart, if you are in darkness, or in the power of sin, I bring to you the Son of God, with the promise that He will come in and take charge. As Potiphar took Joseph, will you not take Jesus? Has He not proven himself worthy to be trusted? Come and say, "Jesus shall have entire charge. He is worthy." Think not only of His divine power, but think of His wonderful love; think of His coming from heaven to save you; think of His dying on Calvary and shedding His blood out of intense love for you. Oh, think of it: Christ in heaven loves every one who is given to Him and whom He has made a child of God. "Having loved his own that were in the world, he loved them unto the end."

Must I plead in the name of the love of the crucified Jesus? Must I plead with you Christians and say, "Look at Jesus, the Son of God, your Redeemer," and ask you to make Him overseer over all? Give Him charge of your temper, your heart's affections, your thoughts, your whole being, and He will prove himself worthy of it.

For a time Joseph had been just a common slave, and with the other slaves had served Pharaoh, Alas! Many a Christian has used Christ for his own advancement and comfort, just as he uses everything in the world. He uses father and mother, minister, money, and all else the world will give, to comfort and make him happy. There is danger of his using Christ Jesus in the same way. But oh, brethren, this is not right. You are His house, and He has a right to dwell therein. Will you not come and surrender all and say, "Lord Jesus, I have made Thee overseer over all"?

Secondly, let's consider the measure of that surrender. We read in the 4th verse, "All that he had he put into his hands." Then in verse 5, "And it came to pass from the time that he made him overseer over all that he had"—there you have it the second time—"the Lord blessed the Egyptian's house, and the blessing of the Lord was upon all that he had"—there the third time. Then in verse 6, "And he left all that he had"—there you have the words the fourth time—"in Joseph's hand, and he knew not all he had, save the bread which he did eat." What do I see here? That Potiphar actually gave everything into Joseph's hands. He made him master over his slaves. All the money was put into Joseph's hands, for we read that Potiphar had care of nothing. When dinner was brought upon the table, he ate of it, and that was all he knew of what was going on in his house. Is not this entire surrender? He gives up everything into the hands of Joseph.

Ah, beloved Christians, I want you to ask yourselves, "Have I done that?" You have offered more than one consecration prayer, and you have more than once said, "Jesus, all I have I give to Thee." You have said it and meant it, but you probably did not realize fully its implications.

With the word surrender there seems always to be a larger and more comprehensive meaning. When surrendering, we do not always succeed in carrying out our intentions, so afterward we take back one thing and another until we have lost sight of our original intention. Beloved Christians, let Christ Jesus have all. Let Him have your whole heart, with its affections. He himself loves with more than the love of Jonathan. Let Him have your whole heart, saying, "Jesus, every fiber of my being, every power of my soul, be devoted to Thee." He will accept that surrender. He spoke a solemn word, "You must hate father and mother." Say today, "Lord Jesus, my love for father and mother, for wife and child, for brother and sister, I give up to Thee. Teach Thou me how to love Thee. I have only one desire, which is to love Thee. I want to give my whole heart to be full of Thy love."

But when you have given your heart, there is yet more to give. There is the head —the brain with its thoughts. I believe Christians do not know how much they rob Christ of in reading so much of the literature of the world. They are often so occupied with their newspapers that the Bible gets a very small place. Oh, friends, I beseech you bring this noble power which God has given you, the power of a mind that can think heavenly, eternal, and infinite things, and lay it at the feet of Jesus, saying, "Lord Jesus, every faculty of my being I want to surrender to Thee that Thou shouldst teach me what to think and how to think for Thee and Thy kingdom." Bless God, there are men who have given their intellect to Jesus, and it has been accepted by Him. And in this connection there is my whole outer life. There is my relation to society, my position among men, my association in my own home, with friends and family; there is my money, my time, my business—all these should be put in the hands of Jesus. One cannot know beforehand the blessedness of this surrender, but blessed it surely is.

Come because He is worthy; come because you know you cannot keep things right yourself. Make Christ master over all you have. Give father and mother, wife and child, house and land, and money, all to Jesus, and you will find that in giving all you receive it back an hundredfold.

Thirdly, look at the blessing of the entire surrender. You have here the remarkable words: "And it came to pass from the time that Potiphar made Joseph overseer over all that he had, that the Lord blessed the Egyptian's house for Joseph's sake, and the blessing of the Lord was upon all that he had in the house, and in the field." I ask you Christians, If God did this to that heathen man because he honored Joseph; if God, for Joseph's sake, blessed that Egyptian in this wonderful way, may a Christian not venture to say, "If I put my life into the hands of Jesus, I am sure God will bless all that I have"? Oh, dare to say it. Potiphar trusted Joseph implicitly and absolutely, and there was prosperity everywhere because God was with Joseph.

Beloved friends, if you but surrender everything, depend upon it, the blessing from that time will be yours. There will be a blessing in your inner life and in your outer life as well. He blessed Potiphar in the house, in the field—everywhere.

Oh, Christian, what is that blessing you will get? I cannot tell all, but I can tell you this: if you will come to Christ Jesus and surrender all, the blessing of God will be on all that you have. There will be a blessing for your own soul. "Thou wilt keep him in perfect peace whose mind is stayed on thee." Try that. Trust Jesus for everything, and trust everything to Him and the blessing of God—the sweet rest, the rest of faith—will come upon you. It is all in the hands of Jesus. He will guide you; He will teach you; He will work in you; He will keep you; He will be everything to you. What a blessed rest and freedom from responsibility and from care, because it is all in the hands of Jesus! I do not say trouble and trial will never come; but in the midst of trial and trouble you will have the all-sufficiency of the presence of Jesus to be your comfort, your help, and your guide. Joseph was sold by his brethren, but he saw God in it, and he was quite content. Christ was betrayed by Judas, condemned by Caiaphas, and given over to execution by Pilate; but in all that, Christ saw God, and He was content. Surrender your life, in all its phases, into the hands of Jesus, remembering that the very hairs of your head are numbered, and not a sparrow falls to earth without the Father's notice. Consent now and say, "I will give everything into the hands of Jesus. Whatever happens is His will regarding me. Whether He comes in the light or in the dark, in the storm or on the troubled sea, I will rest in that blessed assurance. I give up my whole life entirely to Him."

In reading the book of Jonah, we find God's hand in each step of Jonah's experience. It was God who sent the storm when Jonah went aboard the ship, who appointed a whale to swallow him, who ordered the whale to cast him out. Then afterwards it was God who caused the hot wind to blow when the sun was sending down its scorching rays, until the soul of Jonah was grieved. It was God who made the gourd to grow, and later the worm to kill the gourd, and the sea-wind to dry the gourd up quickly. Do we not thus see that every circumstance of our living, every comfort and every trial, comes from God in Christ? There is nothing that can touch a hair of my head. Not a sharp word comes against me, not an unexpected flurry surrounds me, but it is all from Jesus. With my life in His hands, I need care for nothing. I can be content with what Jesus gives.

God blessed Potiphar in the field, in the visible life outside of his house. And God will bless you that, in your association with men, you may be a blessing; that by your holy, humble, respectful, quiet walk, you may carry comfort; that by your loving readiness to be a servant and a helper to all, you may prove what the Spirit of God has done within you. Oh, my brother, my sister, you have no conception of it—I have not—how God is willing to bless the soul utterly given up to Jesus. God can delight in nothing but Jesus. God delights infinitely in Jesus. God longs to see nothing in us but Jesus, and if I give up my heart and life to Jesus, and say, "My God, I want that Thou shouldst see in me nothing but Jesus," then I bring to the Father the sacrifice that is the most acceptable of all. Oh, believers, come today; come out of all your troubles, all your self-efforts, all your self-confidence, and let the blessed Son of God take possession.

Lastly, let me direct your thoughts to the duration of this surrender. I want to emphasize this because in many cases the surrender does not last. Some go away, and

for a time have much gladness and joy,
but it soon begins to decrease, and in a
few weeks or perhaps months it is all gone.
Others who do not lose it entirely complain
sadly at times that it goes away and comes
again. They say, "My life has been very
much blessed since that surrender I made
to God, but it has not always been on the
same level." What did Potiphar do? We
read in the 4th verse, "He made him overseer over his house, and all that he had
he left in Joseph's hands." What a simple
word! He left it there.

And oh, children of God, if you will only
get to that point and say, "For all eternity
I leave it in the hands of Jesus," you will
find what a blessing it is. Potiphar found
now that he could do the king's business
with two hands and an undivided heart. I
might try to rescue a drowning man by
holding fast somewhere with one hand,
while reaching out the other hand to the
man. But it is a grand thing for a person
to be able to stretch out both hands, and
that person is the one who has left all with
Jesus—all his inner life, all his cares and
troubles, and has given himself up entirely
to do the will of God. Will you leave it
there? I must press this because I know
temptations will come. One temptation
will be that the feelings you had in your

act of surrender will pass away; they will not be so bright; another, that circumstances will tempt you. Beloved, temptations will come but God means it for your good. Every temptation brings you a blessing. Do understand that. Learn the lesson of giving up everything to Jesus and letting Jesus take charge of all. Leave it with Jesus. Do not think that by a surrender today or on any day, however powerful, however mighty, things will keep right themselves. Every morning when God wakes you up afresh out of sleep, you need to put your heart, your life, your house, and your business into the hands of Jesus. Wait on Him, if need be, in silence, or in prayer, until He gives you the assurance, "My child, for today all is safe: I take charge." And morning by morning He will renew to you the blessing, and morning by morning you will go out from your quiet time in the consciousness, "Today I have had fellowship with my King, and it is all right." Jesus has taken charge. And so, day by day, you can have grace to leave all in the hands of Jesus.

In conclusion, let me speak to two classes. There are times when your heart is restless; there are times when you are afraid to die.

There are some true believers who have

perhaps never yet understood that it was their duty to surrender everything to Christ. Beloved fellow Christians, I come with a message from your Father: come today and take that word into your hearts and upon your lips even though you do not understand it. "Jesus, I make Thee master of everything, and I will wait at Thy feet that Thou may show me what Thou wouldst have me be and do." Do it now.

Now let me say to believers who have done it before, and who long with an unutterable longing to do it fully and perfectly. Child of God, you can do it, for the Holy Spirit has been sent down from heaven for this one purpose: to glorify Jesus—to glorify Jesus in your heart, by letting you see how perfectly He can take possession of the whole heart; to glorify Jesus by bringing Him into your very life that your whole life may shine out with the glory of Jesus. Depend upon it. The Father will give it to you by the Holy Spirit if you are ready. Oh, come and let your commitment to God be summed up in a simple prayer and answer: "My God, as much as Thou wilt have of me to fill with Christ, Thou shalt have today." "My child, as much of Christ as thy heart longeth to have, thou shalt have; for it is My delight that My Son be in the hearts of My children."

## 9

## Dead with Christ

*Galatians 2:20—I am crucified with Christ.*

The Revised Version properly has the above text, "I have been crucified with Christ." In this connection, let us read the story of a man who was literally crucified with Christ. We may use all the narrative of Christ's work upon earth in the flesh as a type of His spiritual work. Let us take in this instance the story of the penitent thief, Luke 23:39-43, for I think we may learn from him how to live as men who are crucified with Christ. Paul says, "I have been crucified with Christ." And again, "God forbid that I should glory, save in the cross of our Lord Jesus Christ, through whom I have been crucified to the world, and the world to me." We often ask earnestly, "How can I be free from the self life?" The answer is, "Get another life." We often speak about the power of the Holy Spirit coming upon us, but I doubt if we fully realize that the Holy Spirit is a heaven-

ly life come to expel the selfish, fleshly,
earthly life. If we want, in very deed, to
enjoy fully the rest that there is in Jesus,
we can have it only as He comes in, in
the power of His death, to slay what is in
us of nature, and to take possession and
to live His own life in the fullness of the
Holy Ghost. God's Word takes us to the
cross of Christ and teaches us two things.
It tells us that Christ died *for* sin. We understand what that means: in His atonement
He died as I never die, as I never can die,
as I never need die. He died for sin and
for me. But what gave His death such power
to atone? The spirit in which He died, not
the physical suffering, not the external act
of death, but the spirit in which He died.
And what was that spirit? He died *unto*
sin. Sin had tempted Him, surrounded Him,
and had brought Him very nigh to saying,
"I cannot die." In Gethsemane He cried,
"Father, is it not possible that the cup pass
from Me?" But God be praised, He gave
up His life rather than yield to sin. He died
to sin, and in dying He conquered. Now
I cannot die *for* sin like Christ, but I can
and I must die *to* sin like Christ. Christ
died for me. In that He stands alone. Christ
died to sin, and in that I have fellowship
with Him. I have been crucified, I am dead.
And here is the great subject to which

I want to lead you: What it is to be dead with Christ and how I can practically enter into this death with Christ. We know that the great characteristic of Christ is His death. From eternity He came with the commandment of the Father that He should lay down His life on earth. He gave himself up to it, and He set His face towards Jerusalem. He chose death, and He lived and walked upon earth to prepare himself to die. His death is the power of redemption; death gave Him His victory over sin; death gave Him His resurrection, His new life, His exaltation, and His everlasting glory. The great mark of Christ is His death. Even in heaven, upon the throne, He stands as the Lamb that was slain, and through eternity they ever sing, "Thou art worthy, for thou wast slain."

Beloved brother, your Boaz, your Christ, your all-sufficient Saviour, is a Man of whom the chief mark and the greatest glory is this: He died. And if the Bride is to live with her husband as His wife, then she must enter into His state, and into His spirit, and into His disposition, and ever be as He is. If we are to experience the full power of what Christ can do for us, we must learn to die with Christ. Perhaps I shouldn't use the expression, "We must learn to die with Christ." I should rather say, "We must learn that we *are dead* with Christ." That is a glorious thought in the 6th chapter of Romans. To every believer in the Church of Rome—not to the select ones, or the advanced ones, but to every believer in the Church of Rome, however feeble, Paul writes, "You *are dead* with Christ." On the strength of that he says, "Reckon yourselves dead unto sin."

What does it mean to be dead to sin? We cannot see it more clearly than by referring to Adam. Christ was the second Adam. What happened in the first Adam? I died in the first Adam: I died to God; I died in sin. When I was born, I had in me the life of Adam, which had all the characteristics of the life of Adam after he had fallen. Adam died to God and he died in sin, and I inherit the life of Adam, so like him I am dead in sin and dead unto God. But at the very moment I begin to believe in Jesus, I become united to Christ, the second Adam, and as really as I am united by my birth to the first Adam, I am made partaker of the life of Christ. What life? That life which died unto sin on Calvary, and which rose again; therefore God by His apostle tells us, "Reckon yourselves indeed dead unto sin and alive unto God in Christ Jesus." You are to reckon it as true because God says it—for your new nature is indeed, in virtue of your vital union to Christ, actually and utterly dead to sin.

If we want to have the real Christ that God has given us, the real Christ that died for us, in the power of His death and resurrection, we must take our stand here. But many Christians do not understand what the 6th chapter of the Epistle to the Romans teaches us. They do not know that they are dead to sin. They do not know it, and therefore Paul instructs them, "Know ye not that as many of you as are baptized into Christ Jesus, are baptized into his death?" How can we who are dead to sin in Christ live any longer therein? We have indeed the death and the life of Christ working within us. But, alas! most Christians do not know this, and therefore do not experience or practice it. They need to be taught that their first need is to be brought to the recognition, to the knowledge, of what has taken place in Christ on Calvary, and what has taken place in their becoming united to Christ. The man must begin to say, even before he understands it, "In Christ I am dead to sin." It is a command: "Reckon ye yourselves indeed to be dead unto sin." Get hold of your union to Christ; believe in the new nature within you, that spiritual life which you have from Christ, a life that has died and been raised again.

A man's acts are always in accordance with his idea of his state. A king acts like a king, otherwise we say, "That man has forgotten his kingship," but if a man is conscious of being a king, he behaves like a king. And so I cannot live the life of a true believer unless I am filled with a consciousness of this every day, "I thank God that I am dead in Christ. Christ died unto sin, and since I am united with Christ, and Christ lives in me I am dead to sin."

What is the life that Christ lives in me? Before that question can be answered ask, what is the life that Adam lives in me? Adam lives in me the death life, a life that has fallen under the power of sin and death, death to God. That life Adam lives in me by nature as an unconverted man. And Christ, the second Adam, has come to me with a new life, and I now live in His life, the death-life of Christ. But as long as I do not know it, I cannot act according to it, though it be in me. Praise God, when a man begins to see what it is, and begins in obedience to say, "I will do what God's Word says; I am dead, I reckon myself dead," he enters upon a new life. On the strength of God's everlasting Word and your union to Christ and the great fact of Calvary, reckon—know yourself as dead indeed unto sin. A man must see this truth; this is the first step.

The second is that he must accept it in faith. And what then? When he accepts it in faith, then there comes in him a struggle and a painful experience, for that faith is still very feeble. He begins to ask, "But why, if I am dead to sin, do I commit so much sin?" And the answer God's Word gives is simply this: You do not allow the power of that death to be applied by the Holy Spirit. What we need is to understand that the Holy Spirit came from heaven, from the glorified Jesus, to bring His death and His life into us. The two are inseparably connected: That Christ died, He died unto sin, and that He liveth, He liveth unto God. Death and life in Him are inseparable; even so in us the life to God in Christ is inseparably connected with the death to sin. And that is what the Holy Ghost will teach us and work in us. If I have accepted Christ in faith by the Holy Ghost, and yield myself to Him, He will keep possession and reveal the full power of my fellowship in His death and life in my heart every day. To some this undoubtedly comes in one moment of supreme power and blessing; all at once they see and accept it, and enter in, and there is death to sin as a divine experience. It is not that the tendency to evil is rooted out. No. It is that the power of Christ's death keeps one from sin; it destroys the power of sin. The power of Christ's death

can be manifested in the Holy Spirit's unceasingly mortifying the deeds of the body.

Someone asks me if there is still growth
needed. Undoubtedly. By the Holy Spirit
a man can now begin to live and grow,
deeper and deeper, into the fellowship of
Christ's death. New things are discovered
by him in spheres he never thought. A man
may at times be filled with the Holy Ghost
and yet imperfections be found in him.
Why? Because his heart, perhaps, had not
been fully prepared by a complete dis-
covery of sin. There may be pride, or self-
consciousness, or forwardness, or other
qualities of this nature which he has never
noticed. The Holy Spirit does not always
cast these out at once. No. There are different ways of entering into the blessed
life. One man enters into the blessed life
with the idea of power for service; another
with the idea of rest from worry and
weariness; another with the idea of deliverance from sin. In all these aspects there
is something limited; therefore every believer is to give himself up after he knows
the power of Christ's death, and say continually, "Lord Jesus, let the power of
Thy death work through; let it penetrate
my whole being." As the man gives himself
unreservedly up, he will begin to bear
the marks of a crucified man. The apostle

says, "I have been crucified," and he lives
like a crucified man.

What are the marks of a crucified man?
The first is deep, absolute humility. Christ
humbled himself and became obedient unto
death, even the death of the cross. When
the death to sin begins to work mightily,
that is one of its chief and most blessed
proofs. It breaks a man down, down, and
the great longing of his heart is, "Oh,
that I could get deeper down before my
God, and be nothing at all, that the life of
Christ might be exalted. I deserve nothing
but the cursed cross; I give myself over
to it." Humility is one of the great marks
of a crucified man.

Another mark is impotence, helplessness. When a man hangs on the cross, he
is utterly helpless; he can do nothing. As
long as we Christians are strong, and
can work, or struggle, we do not get into
the blessed life of Christ; but when a man
says, "I am a crucified man, I am utterly
helpless, every breath of life and strength
must come from my Jesus," then we learn
what it is to sink into our own impotence
and say, "I am nothing."

Still another mark of crucifixion is rest-
fulness. Yes. Christ was crucified, and went
down into the grave, and we are crucified
and buried with Him. There is no place of

rest like the grave; a man can do nothing there. "My flesh shall rest in hope," said David and the Messiah. Yes, and when a man goes down into the grave of Jesus, it means this: that he just cries out, "I have nothing but God, I trust God; I am waiting upon God; my flesh rests in Him; I have given up everything that I may rest, waiting upon what God is to do to me."

Remember, the crucifixion, the death, and the burial are inseparably one. Remember also that the grave is the place where the mighty resurrection power of God will be manifested. John 11 says, "Said I not unto thee"—when did Christ say that? It was at the grave of Lazarus—"that if thou believest, thou shalt see the glory of God?" Where shall I see the glory of God most brightly? Beside the grave. Go down into death believing, and the glory of God will come upon thee and fill thy heart.

Dear friends, we want to die. If we are to live in the rest, and the peace, and the blessedness of our great Boaz; if we are to live a life of joy and of fruitfulness, of strength and of victory, we must go down into the grave with Christ, and the language of our life must be: "I am a crucified man. God be praised, though I have nothing but sin in myself, I have an everlasting Jesus, with His death and His life, to be the life of my soul."

How can I enter into this fellowship of the cross? We find an illustration in the story of the penitent thief. Thomas said, before Christ's death, "Let us go and abide with him." And Peter said, "Lord, I am ready to go with thee to prison, or to death." But the disciples all failed, and our Lord took a man who was the offscouring of the earth and hung him upon the cross of Calvary beside himself, and He said to Peter and to all, "I will let you see what it is to die with Me."

And He says that word today to the weakest and the humblest; if you are longing to know what it is to enter into death with Jesus, come and look at the penitent thief. And what do we see there? First of all, we see the state of a heart prepared to die with Christ. We see in that penitent thief, a humble, wholehearted confession of sin. There he hung upon the cursed tree, with the multitudes blaspheming the man beside him, but he was not ashamed to make confession publicly. "I am dying a death that I have deserved. I am suffering justly; this cross is what I have deserved." Here is one of the reasons why the Church of Christ enters so little into the death of Christ; men do not want to believe that the curse of God is upon everything in them that has not died with Christ. People talk about the curse of sin, but they do not understand that the whole nature has been infected by sin, and that the curse is on everything.

My intellect, has that been defiled by sin? Terribly, and the curse of sin is on it; therefore my intellect must go down into the death. Ah, I believe that the Church of Christ suffers more today from trusting in intellect, in sagacity, in culture, and in mental refinement, than from almost anything else. The Spirit of the world comes in, and men seek by their wisdom and knowledge to help the Gospel, but they rob it of its crucifixion mark. Christ directed Paul to go and preach the gospel of the cross, but to do it not with wisdom of words.

The curse of sin is on all that is of nature. If there be a minister who has delighted in preaching, who has done his very best, who has given his very best in the way of talent and of thought, and who asks, "Must that go down into the grave?" I say, "Yes, my brother, the whole man must be crucified." And so with the heart's affection. What is more beautiful than the love of a child for his mother? In that lovely nature there is something unsanctified, and it must be given up to die. God will raise it from the dead and give it back again, sanctified and made alive unto God. So we might go through the whole of our life. People often say to me, "But has God made all things so beautiful, and is it not right that we should enjoy them? Are not His gifts all good?" I answer yes, but remember what it says: they are good if sanctified by the Word of God and prayer. The curse of sin is on them; the blight of sin is on everything most beautiful, and it takes much of God's Word and prayer to sanctify them. It is very hard to give up a thing to the death, especially one's life, and we never will until we have learned that everything about that life is stamped by sin, and let it go down into the death as the only way to have it quickened and sanctified.

The penitent thief confessed his sin and that he deserved death. Then, next, he had a wonderful faith in the almighty power of Christ. It has no parallel in the Bible. There hangs the cursed malefactor with Jesus of Nazareth, and he dares speak and say, "I am dying here under the just curse of my sins, but I believe Thou canst take me into Thy heart and remember me when Thou comest into Thy kingdom."

Oh, that we might learn to believe in the almighty power of Christ! That man believed that Christ was a King and had a kingdom, and that He would take him up in His arms and in His heart and remember

him when He came into His kingdom. He
believed that, and believing that, he died.

Brother, you and I need to take time to
come to a much larger and deeper faith in
the power of Christ, that the almighty
Christ will indeed take us in His arms and
carry us through this death life, revealing
the power of His death in us. I cannot live
it without personal contact with Christ every hour of the day. Christ must do it;
Christ *can* do it. Come therefore and say,
"Is He not the almighty One? Did He not
come from the throne of God? Did He not
prove His omnipotence, and did the Father
not prove it when He rose from the dead?"
Now that Christ is on the throne, would you
be afraid to do what the malefactor did
when Christ was upon the cross, and
entrust yourself to Him to live as one dead
with Him? Christ will carry you through
the very process He went through. He will
make His death work in you every day of
your life.

I note one thing more in the penitent
thief—his prayer. There was his conviction
of sin and his faith, but there was, further,
the utterance of his faith in prayer. He
turned to Jesus. Remember that the whole
world, with perhaps the exception of Mary
and the women, was turned against Christ
that day. Of the whole world of men as

far as I know, there was but that one praying to Christ. Do not wait to see what others
do; if you wait for that—alas! I desire to
say it in love and tenderness—you will not
find much company in the Church of Christ.
Pray incessantly, "Lord Christ, let the
power of Thy death come into me." For
God's sake, pray the prayer. If you want
to live the life of heaven, there must be
death to sin in the power of Jesus. There
must be personal entrustment of the soul
into His death to sin, a personal acceptance
of Jesus to do the mighty work.

We have seen what the preparation was
on the part of this man. Let us look, secondly, at how Christ met him. He met him with
that wonderful promise, with its three
wonderful parts: "Today shalt thou be with
me in Paradise." It was a promise of fellowship with Christ—"Thou shalt be with me";
a promise of rest in eternity, in the Paradise from which sin had cast man out—
"with me in Paradise"; a promise of immediate blessing—"Today shalt thou be
with me."

With that threefold blessing Jesus comes
to you and me, and He says, "Believer,
are you longing to live the Paradise life
where I give souls to eat of the Tree of
Life, in the Paradise of God, day by day?
Are you longing for the uninterrupted

communion with God that there was in
Paradise before Adam fell? Are you longing for perfect fellowship with Me, longing
to live where I am living, in the love of the
Father? Today, today, even as the Holy
Ghost says, 'Today shalt thou be with
me!' Longest thou for Me? I long more for
thee. Longest thou for fellowship? I long
unceasingly for thy fellowship, for I need
thy love, My child, to satisfy My heart.
Nothing can prevent My receiving thee into
fellowship. I have taken possession of
heaven for thee, as the Great High Priest,
that thou mightest live the heavenly life,
that thou mightest have access into the
holiest of all and an abiding dwelling place
there. Today, if thou wilt, thou shalt be with
me in Paradise."

Thank God, the Jesus of the penitent
thief is my Jesus. Thank God, the cross of
the penitent thief is my cross. I must confess my sinfulness if I want to come into
the closest communion with my blessed
Lord. During the thirty-three years of
Christ's life, there was not a man upon
earth that had such wonderful fellowship
with the Son of God as the penitent thief,
for with the Son of God he entered glory.
What made him so separate from others?
He was on the cross with Jesus and entered
Paradise with Him. And if I live upon the

cross with Jesus, the Paradise life shall be mine every day.

And now, if Jesus gives me that promise, what have I to do? Let go. When a ship is moored alongside the dock, with everything ready for the start and all standing on the quay, the last bell is rung and the order is given, "Let go." Then the last rope is loosened, and the steamer moves. Likewise there are things that tie us to the earth, to the flesh-life and to the self-life; but today the message comes: "If thou wouldst die with Jesus, let go." Thou needst not understand all. It may not be perfectly clear; the heart may appear dull, but never mind; Jesus carried that penitent thief through death to life. The thief did not know where he was going; he did not know what was to happen; but Jesus, the mighty conqueror, took him in His arms and landed him in his ignorance, in Paradise.

Oh, I have sometimes said in my soul, bless God for the ignorance of that penitent thief. He knew nothing about what was going to happen, but he trusted Christ. And if I cannot understand all about this crucifixion with Christ—death to sin, the life to God, and the glory that comes into the heart—never mind, I trust my Lord's promise. I cast myself helplessly into His arms. I maintain my position on the cross. Given up to Jesus to die with Him, I can trust Him to carry me through.

Shall we not each one take the blessed opportunity of doing what Ruth did when she, in obedience to the advice of her mother, just cast herself at the feet of the great Boaz, the Redeemer, to be His? Shall we not come into personal contact with Jesus, and shall not each one of us just speak before the world these simple words: "Lord, here is this life; there is much in it still of self, and sinfulness, and self-will, but I come to Thee. I long to enter fully into Thy death. I long to know fully that I have been crucified with Thee. I long to live Thy life every day." Then say, "Lord Jesus, I have seen Thy glory, what Thou didst for the penitent one at Thy side on the cross; I am trusting Thee that Thou wilt do it for me. Lord, I cast myself into Thy arms."

## 10

## Joy in the Holy Ghost

*Romans 14:17—For the kingdom of God is not meat and drink, but righteousness, and peace, and joy in the Holy Ghost.*

In this text we have the earthly revelation of the work of the Trinity. The Kingdom of God is righteousness; that represents the work of the Father. The foundations of His throne are justice and judgment. Then comes the work of the Son: He is our peace, our Shiloh, our rest. The Kingdom of God is peace—not only the peace of pardon for the past, but the peace of perfect assurance for the future. Not only is the work of atonement in Christ finished, but the work of sanctification is also finished, and I may receive and enjoy what is prepared for me. The new man has been created, and I may in Him live out my life. If a kingdom is established in righteousness, if the rule is perfect, there can be perfect rest. If there be peace—no war from without and no civil dissension within—a nation can be happy and prosperous.

And so there comes here, after righteousness and peace, the joy, the blessed happiness, in which a man can live: "The kingdom of God is righteousness, and peace, and joy in the Holy Ghost." May we regard this joy of the Holy Ghost, not only as a beautiful thing to admire, not only as a thing to have beautiful thoughts about, but as a blessing that we are going to claim.

We often see a confectioner's shop, with beautiful fruit or cake temptingly displayed in the window. There is a great pane of plate glass before it, and the hungry little boys stand there and look, and long, but they cannot reach it. If you were to say to one, "Now, little boy, take that fruit," he would look at you in surprise. He has learned that there is something between. If he had never known of glass, he might attempt it. The plate glass is sometimes so clear that even a grown man might for a moment be deceived and stretch out his hand. But he soon finds there is something invisible between him and the fruit. This represents exactly the life of many Christians: they see but they cannot take.

What now is this invisible pane of plate glass that hinders my taking the beautiful things I see? It is nothing but the self-life. I see divine things but cannot reach them; the self-life is the invisible plate glass. We are willing, we are working, we are striving, and yet we are holding back something; we are afraid to give up everything to God. We do not know what the consequences may be. We have not yet comprehended that God and Christ Jesus are worth everything. Whatever is told us of the blessed life of peace and joy, we say, "Praise God. God's Word is true; I believe the Word"; and yet, day by day, we stand back. When someone says, "Take it," we say, "I can't take it; there is something between." Oh, that we were willing to give up the self-life, that we had the courage to give up today and let the joy of the Holy Ghost be our religion. That is the religion God has prepared for us; that is the religion we can claim—not only righteousness, not only peace, but the joy of the Holy Ghost. That is the Kingdom of God.

What is this joy? First of all, it is the joy of the presence of Jesus. We are often inclined to speak most of two other things: the power for sanctification and the power for service. But I find there is something more important than either of those two, and that is that the Holy Ghost came from heaven to be the abiding presence of Christ in His disciples, in the Church, and in the heart of every believer. The Lord Jesus was

going away, and His disciples were very
sad. Their hearts were sorrowful, but He
said to them, "I will come back again, and
I will come to you. Your hearts shall rejoice, and your joy no man shall take from
you." What took place with them may take
place with us too. The Holy Spirit is given
to make the presence of Jesus an abiding
reality, a continual experience. And what
was that joy that no man could ever touch?
It was the joy of Pentecost. And what was
Pentecost? The coming of the Lord Jesus
in the Holy Ghost to dwell with His disciples. While Jesus was with His disciples
on earth, He could not get into their hearts
in the right way. They loved Him, but they
could not take in His teaching, they could
not partake of His disposition, and they
could not receive His very spirit into their
being. But when He had ascended to heav-
en, He came back in the Spirit to dwell
in their hearts. It is this alone that will
help us to go—the minister to his congregation with its difficulties; the business
man to his counter; the mother to her large
family with its care; the worker to her Bible
class. It is this only that will help us to
feel, "I can conquer, I can live in the rest
of God." Why? "Because I have the almighty Jesus with me every day."

With God's people, there seems to be one

hindrance: *they do not know their Saviour.*
They do not realize that this blessed Christ
is an ever-present, all-pervading, indwelling
Christ, who wants to take charge of their
entire lives. They do not know, they do not
believe, that He is an almighty Christ and
ready in the midst of any difficulties and
any circumstances to be their keeper and
their God. This is absolutely true.

Many Christians are asked as to how
one may have the joy unspeakable, the joy
that nothing can take away, the joy of the
friendship and nearness and love of Jesus
filling his heart. We complain that the rush
of competition is so terrible that we cannot
find time for private prayer. Brother, the
Lord Jesus Christ, if He comes to you as
a brother and a friend and an abiding guest,
can give your heart the joy of the Holy
Ghost so that business will take its right
place under your feet. Your heart is too
holy to have it filled with business; let the
business be in the head and under the feet,
but let Christ have the whole heart, and
He will keep the whole life.

Our glorious, exalted, almighty, ever-
present Christ! Why is it that you and I
cannot trust Him fully, perfectly to do His
work? Shall we not say before God that
we do trust Him, that we will trust Christ
to be to us every moment all that we can

desire? On the cross of Calvary Christ was all alone, and you believe He did a perfect and a blessed work. And Christ in heaven is all alone, as high priest and intercessor, and you trust Him for His work there. But, praise God, it is equally true that Christ in the heart is able all alone to keep it all the days. May it please God to reveal to His children the nearness of Christ standing and knocking at the door of every heart, ready to come in and rest forever there and to lead the soul into His rest.

We all know what the power of joy is. There is nothing so attractive as joy, there is nothing that can help a man to bear and endure so much as joy. The Lord Jesus himself for the joy that was set before Him endured the cross. One is not living aright if he is living a sighing, trembling, doubting life. Come today and believe the joy of the Holy Ghost is meant for you. Does not the Scripture say, "Whom not having seen we love; in whom though now ye see him not, yet believing ye rejoice with joy unspeakable and full of glory"? Do you not believe that this blessed, adorable, inconceivably beautiful Son of God, the delight of the Father, could fill your heart with delight day and night if He were always present? And do you not believe that

He loves you more than a bridegroom loves his bride? Do you not believe that, having bought you with His blood, Jesus is longing for you? He needs you to satisfy His heart of love. Begin to believe with your whole heart, "The joy of the Holy Ghost is my portion, for the Holy Ghost secures to me without interruption the presence and the love of Jesus."

Secondly, there is the joy of deliverance from sin. The Holy Ghost comes to sanctify us. Christ is our sanctification, and the Holy Ghost comes to communicate Him to us, to work out all that is in Christ and to reproduce it in us. Let us remember that in the sight of God there is something more than work. There is Christlikeness—the likeness and the life of Christ in us. That is what God wants; that will fit us for work. God asks not that Christ should live in us as separate persons—temples full of filthy, impure, foul creatures, with Christ hidden away somewhere there. That is not the intention of God. He wants Christ so formed in us that we are one with Christ, and that in our thinking, feeling and living, the image of His blessed Son is manifest before Him. The Holy Spirit is given to sanctify us.

My brother, are you willing to be sanctified from every sin, be that sin great or

small? I am not asking, do you feel that
you have the power to conquer it? I am
not even asking, do you feel the power to
cast it out? It may be that you feel no
power; that won't hinder if you are willing.
I cannot cast out sin, but I can get the
almighty Christ by the Holy Spirit to do it,
and it is my work to say to Christ, "There
is the sin, there is the evil thing. I lay it
at Thy feet. I cast it there, I cast it into
Thy very bosom. Lord, I am ready to cut
off the right hand, anything, only deliver
me from it." Then Christ will cast out the
evil spirit and give deliverance. The Spirit
of God is a holy spirit and His work is to
make free from the power of sin and death.
And if you want to live in the joy of the
Holy Ghost, the question comes: "Are you
willing to surrender everything that is sinful, even what appears good, but has the
stain of sin on it?" You may be involved
in relationships that make your life very
difficult. A pastor with his people may be
brought into very difficult relationships; or
a businessman with his partner, or those
with whom he has to associate, may be in
an exceedingly trying position. But is not
the blessed Lamb of God worth it all? What
is the Christ worth to you? The question
was once asked the disciples, "What think
ye of Christ?" I ask, "What is Christ worth

to you?" And I beseech you, whatever prospective difficulties there may be, and whatever perplexities surround you, take the whole world today and cast it at His feet. To have Him is worth any difficulty; to have Him will be the solution to every difficulty.

There are not only external, manifest difficulties and perplexities, but there are a thousand little things that come into our life and disturb us, such as temptations to unloving feelings, and sharp words, and hasty judgments. Oh, come, and believe that the Holy Spirit, the sanctifier, can come in and rule and give grace to pass through all without sinning, and you shall know what the joy of the Holy Ghost is. Our body, we read in First Corinthians, is the temple of the Holy Ghost. It is to be holy in things like eating and drinking. How often a Christian comes to the consciousness that he takes or seeks too much enjoyment in eating, eating for pleasure, with no self-denial or self-sacrifice in his feeding the body! How often we tempt one another to eat, and how often the believer forgets that this body is the very secret temple of the Holy Ghost and that every mouthful we eat and drink must be for the glory of God in such a way as to be perfectly well pleasing to Him!

Beloved, I bring you a message: There

is access for you into the rest of God, and
the Holy Spirit is given to bring you in.
He will fill your heart with the unutterable
joy of Christ's presence, with the joy of
deliverance from sin, of victory over sin;
the unutterable joy of knowing that you are
doing God's will and are pleasing in His
sight; the unutterable joy of knowing that
He is sanctifying and keeping the temple
for Christ to dwell in. Believers, the joy of
the Holy Ghost, the joy of that holiness of
God, is His blessedness, His purity, His
perfection, that nothing can mar or stain
or disturb. The Holy Ghost waits to bring
and to manifest it in our lives. He wants
to so come into our hearts that we shall
live, as Holy Ghost men, the sanctified
life, with the sanctifying power of Jesus
running through our whole beings.

My third thought is: The joy of the
Holy Ghost is the joy of the love of the
saints. At Pentecost the Holy Ghost was not
given to any man separate from the others;
He came and filled the whole company.
We know how much division and separation
and pride there had been among them, but
on that day the Holy Ghost so filled their
hearts that we find it was afterward said,
"Behold how these men love one another."
There was a love in the primitive church
that the very heathen noticed and could not

understand. Why was that? The Holy
Spirit is the bond of union between the
Father and Son, and that bond is love. The
Holy Spirit is the love of God come to dwell
in the heart. When He dwells with me and
my brother, we learn to love each other.
Though I be unloving naturally, and though
I have very little grace, if the heart of my
brother is full of the Holy Spirit, he loves
me through it all.

Love is a wonderful thing. As long as
a man tries to love it is not real love, but
when real love comes, the more opposition
it meets the more it triumphs, for the more
it can exercise itself and perfect itself,
the more it rejoices. Take a mother with
a son who dishonors her. How her love fol-
lows him! When she sees that he has fallen
deeper than ever before, how the dear
mother heart only loves him the more intensely through all the wretchedness! Does
not the Scripture say, "If He gave His life
for us, we are bound to give our life for the
brethren"? The Holy Spirit comes as a
spirit of love, and if you want to know the
joy of the Holy Ghost, and want Him to
lead you into the rest of God and keep you
there, beware above everything on earth or
in hell of being unloving. One sharp word
to your brother or sister brings a cloud
upon you without your knowing it. People

are so accustomed to talk just as they like about each other that they say sharp and unkind and unloving things, and when a cloud comes in consequence they cannot understand it. If there is one thing that grieves God, if there is one thing that hinders the Spirit—the fruit of the Spirit is love—it is the lack of lovingness.

If you want to live in the joy of the Holy Ghost, make your covenant with God. "But," you say, "there is a Christian man who makes me so impatient; he does trouble me and vex me so with his stupidity. And there are those worldly men; how they have tempted me in times past and done me harm! And there is that business-man who is trying to ruin me." Take them all, and your own wife and children and everyone around you and say, "I understand it, love is rest and rest is love. God resteth in His love. Love is rest and rest is love, and where there is no love the rest must be disturbed."

Let us say today, "I see what joy is. It is the joy of always loving; it is the joy of losing my own life in love to others." In connection with humility, someone asks, "How about that text, 'In honor preferring one another'?" When a soul comes into perfect humility before God, it becomes nothing and God becomes all in all. I am nothing. There is no self to be affronted. I have said before God, "I am nothing; it is only Thy life and light that shines. The honor is Thine, and nothing may touch me but what it first touches my God."

Beloved, are you living in the joy of the Holy Ghost? Come and accept a blessing and give yourself up to live a life of humility in which you are nothing, and a life of love like Christ's in which you only live for your fellowmen, for the Kingdom of God is the joy of the Holy Ghost.

My last thought is that the joy of the Holy Ghost is the joy of working for God. We have considered the joy of the presence of Jesus, the joy of deliverance from sin, the joy of love for the brethren. Now we're talking about the joy of working for God. Some of us have at times felt what an incomprehensible thing it is that the everlasting God should work through us, and we have said, "Lord, what is this, that Thou, the almighty One, dost work in me and through me, a vile worm by nature?" It is a mystery that passeth knowledge, and yet it is so true. The joy of the Holy Ghost comes when a man gives himself up to the Christlike work of carrying the love of God to men. Let us seek the perishing; let us live and die for souls; let us live and die that our fellowmen may be reclaimed and

brought back to their God. There is no joy
like hearing the joy-song of a new-born
soul.

Yet, there is another joy that may be
as deep. Even if God does not give me the
blessing of hearing the new-born soul sing
its song, I may have the joy, the sympathy
with Jesus in His rejected life, and the assurance that the Father looks with good
pleasure on me. When I think of the thousands of believers in the Christian world
and then think of the heathen world, the
cry comes up in my heart, "What are we
doing?" Ah, we need to be crying to God
day and night, "Lord God, wake us up.
Lord God, let the Holy Spirit burn within
us."

Are we the true successors of Jesus
Christ? Are we indeed the followers and
successors of Christ who went all the way
to Calvary to give His blood for us? Let
us remember that the joy of the Holy Ghost
is the joy of working for God in Christ. I
believe that God has new ways and new
leadings and new power for His people if
they will only wait on him. But what most
of us do is this: We thank God for all He
has given, we look at all the ways of working we have, and we say that we will try
to do our work better. But oh, if we had
a sense of the need, if we had any sense,

by the vision of the Holy Ghost, of the state of the millions around us, I am sure we would fall on our faces before God and say, "God help me to something new. Oh, that every fiber of my being may be taken possession of for this great work with God!" The great need is that all Christians should consecrate themselves wholly to God for His work. May God help us to know what is the joy of the Holy Ghost.

Concluding, I ask again, "Do you believe that it is possible for the Lord Jesus, our Shiloh, of whom Jacob prophesied, our Joshua, our glorious King and High Priest —do you believe it is possible for Christ Jesus to bring you today into the rest of God? Remember that word in Hebrews, "Even as the Holy Ghost saith, today." Today, summon up courage and take up your ministry, your business, your surroundings, your natural temperament, your home, and your life for the days to come upon earth, and say, "I do not understand it. I know not what will come, but one thing I know, I do absolutely give everything into the hands of the crucified Lamb of God. He shall have me in my entirety." And oh, remember, beloved, that Christ will be to you more than you can think or understand, more than you can ask or desire.

Come, let us cast ourselves into those

blessed, loving arms, and let us believe even now that our Joshua leads us into the rest of God, the rest in which we are saved from self-care, self-seeking, self-trusting, and self-loving, the rest in which we do not think of ourselves, but where we know that He who is almighty and omnipresent will always be with us and working in us. When we have done that, let us claim the promise, that as we have sought first the Kingdom and God's righteousness, all things shall be added unto us. Beloved, the Kingdom of God is within you, and it is righteousness, peace and joy in the Holy Ghost. Come, let us claim it even now in simple, childlike humble faith.

## 11

## Triumph of Faith

*John 4:50—And the man believed the word that Jesus had spoken unto him.*

Let me quote from the Gospel according to St. John, the 4th chapter, beginning at the 46th verse: "So Jesus came again into Cana of Galilee, where he made the water wine. And there was a certain nobleman whose son was sick at Capernaum. When he heard that Jesus was come out of Judea into Galilee, he went unto him, and besought him that he would come down, and heal his son: for he was at the point of death. Then said Jesus unto him, Except ye see signs and wonders, ye will not believe." There you have the word "believe" for the first time in the passage. "The nobleman saith unto him, Sir, come down ere my child die. Jesus saith unto him, Go thy way; thy son liveth. And the man believed the word that Jesus had spoken unto him, and he went his way." There you have that word the second time. "And as he was now going down, his servants met him, and told him, saying, Thy son liveth. Then inquired he of them the hour when he began to amend. And they said unto him, Yesterday at the seventh hour the fever left him. So the father knew that it was at the same hour, in the which Jesus said unto him, Thy son liveth: and himself believed, and his whole house." There you have the word "faith."

This story has often been used to illustrate the different steps of faith in the spiritual life. It was this use of it in an address that brought the sainted Canon Battersby into the full enjoyment of rest. He had been a most godly man but had lived the life of failure. He saw in the story what it was to rest on the Word and trust the saving power of Jesus, and from that night he was a changed man. He went home to testify of it, and under God, he was allowed to originate the Keswick Convention.

Let me point out to you the three aspects of faith which we have here: first, faith seeking; then, faith finding; and then, faith enjoying. Or, still better: faith struggling; faith resting; faith triumphing. First of all, faith struggling. Here is a man, a heathen, a nobleman, who has heard about Christ. He has a dying son at Capernaum, and in his extremity leaves his home and walks some six or seven hours away to Cana of Galilee. He has heard of the Prophet, pos-

sibly, as one who has made water wine;
he has heard of His other miracles round
Capernaum, and he has a certain trust that
Jesus will be able to help him. He goes to
Him, and his prayer is that the Lord will
come down to Capernaum and heal his son.
Christ said to him, "Except ye see signs
and wonders, ye will not believe." He saw
that the nobleman wanted Him to come and
stand beside the child. This man had not
the faith of the centurion, "Only speak a
word." He had a faith, but it was faith that
came from hearsay, and it was faith that
did, to a certain extent, hope in Christ.
However, it was not the faith in Christ's
power such as Christ desired. Still Christ
accepted and met this faith. After the
Lord had thus told him what He wished—
a faith that could fully trust Him—the
nobleman cried the second time, "Sir, come
down ere my child die." Seeing his earnestness and his trust, Christ said, "Go thy
way; thy son liveth." And then we read that
the nobleman believed. He believed, and he
went his way. He believed the word that
Jesus had spoken. In that he rested and
was content. And he went away without
having any other pledge than the word of
Jesus. As he was walking homeward, the
servants met him to tell him his son lived.
He asked at what hour he began to amend.

And when they told him, he knew it was at the very hour that Jesus had been speaking to him.

At first he had a faith that was seeking, struggling, and searching for blessing; then he had a faith that accepted the blessing simply as it was contained in the word of Jesus. When Christ said, "Thy son liveth," he was content, and went home and found the blessing—the son restored.

Then came the third step in his faith. He believed with his whole house. That is to say, he did not only believe that Christ could do just this one thing, the healing of his son; but he believed in Christ as his Lord. He gave himself up entirely to be a disciple of Jesus. And that not only alone, but with his whole house.

Many Christians are like the nobleman. They have heard about a better life. They have met certain individuals by whose Christian lives they have been impressed, and consequently have felt that Christ can do wonderful things for a man. Many Christians say in their heart, "I am sure there is a better life for me to live; how I wish I could be brought to that blessed state!" But they do not have much hope about it. They have read, and prayed, but they have found everything so difficult. If you ask them, "Do you believe Jesus can help you

to live this higher life?" they say, "Yes,
He is omnipotent." If you ask, "Do you
believe Jesus wishes to do it?" they say,
"Yes, I know He is loving." And if you
say, "Do you believe that He will do it for
you?" they at once say, "I know He is
willing, but whether He will actually do it
for me I do not know. I am not sure that
I am prepared. I do not know if I am
advanced enough. I do not know if I have
enough grace for that." And so they
hunger, struggle, wrestle, and often remain
unblessed. This state sometimes goes on for
years—expecting to see signs and wonders
and hoping that God, by a miracle, will put
them all right. They are just like the Israelites: they limit the Holy One of Israel.
Have you ever noticed that it is the very
people whom God has blessed so wonderfully who do that? What did the Israelites
say? "God hath provided water in the wilderness. But can He provide a table in the
wilderness? We do not think He can."
And so we find believers who say, "Yes,
God has done wonders. The whole of redemption is a wonder, and God has done
wonders for some whom I know. But will
God take one so feeble as I and put me
entirely right?"

The struggling, wrestling, and seeking
are the beginnings of faith in you—a faith

that desires and hopes. But it must go on further. And how can that faith advance? Look at the second step. There is the nobleman. Christ speaks to him this wonderful word, "Go thy way; thy son liveth," and the nobleman simply rests upon the word of the living Jesus. He rests on it, without any proof of what he is to get, and without one man in the world to encourage him. He goes home with the thought, "I have received the blessing I sought. I have received life from the dead for my son. The living Christ promised it me, and on that I rest." The struggling, seeking faith has become a resting faith. The man has entered into rest about his son.

And now, dear believers, this is the one thing God asks you to do: God has said that in Christ you have eternal life, the more abundant life; Christ has said to you, "I live, and ye shall live also." The Word says to us that Christ is our peace, our victory over every enemy, He who leads us into the rest of God. These are the words of God, and His message has come to us that Christ can do for us what Moses could not have done. Moses had no Christ to live in him. But it is told you that you can have what Moses had not: you can have a living Christ within you. Are you going to believe that apart from any experience and apart from any consciousness of strength? If the peace of God is to rule in your heart, it is the God of peace himself who must be there to do it. The peace is inseparable from God. The light of the sun—can I separate that from the sun? Utterly impossible. As long as I have the sun I have the light. If I lose the sun I lose the light. Take care! Do not seek the peace of God or the peace of Christ apart from God and Christ.

But how does Christ come to me? He comes to me in this precious Word; and just as He said to the nobleman, "Go thy way home; thy son liveth," so Christ comes to me today and says, "Go thy way; thy Saviour liveth." "Lo, I am with you alway." "I live, and ye shall live also." "I wait to take charge of your whole life. Will you have Me do this? Trust to Me all that is evil and feeble—your whole sinful and perverse nature. Give it to Me—that dying, sin-sick soul. Give it up to Me and I will take care of it."

Will you not listen and hear Him speak to your soul: "Child, go forward into all the circumstances of life that have tempted you; into all the difficulties that threaten you"? Your soul lives with the life of God; your soul lives in the power of God; your soul lives in Christ Jesus. Will you not, like the nobleman, take the simple step of faith and believe the word Jesus hath spoken? Will you not say, "Lord Jesus, Thou hast spoken: I can rest on Thy Word. I have seen that Christ is willing to be more to me than I ever knew. I have seen that Christ is willing to be my life in the most actual and intense meaning of the words." All that we know about the Holy Ghost sums itself up in this one thing: The Holy Ghost comes to make Christ an actual, indwelling, always-abiding Saviour.

Lastly comes the triumphant faith. The man went home holding fast the promise. He had only one promise, but he held it fast. When God gives me a promise, He is just as near me as when He fulfills it. That is a great comfort. When I have the promise I have also the pledge of the fulfillment. But the whole heart of God is just as much in His promise as in the fulfillment of it; and sometimes God, the promiser, is more precious because I am compelled to cling more to Him, to come closer, to live by simple faith, and to adore His love. Do not think this is a hard life, to be living upon a promise. It means living upon the everlasting God. Who is going to say that is hard? It means living upon the crucified, the loving Christ. Be ashamed to say that is a difficult thing. It is a blessed thing.

The nobleman went home and found the

child living. What happened then? Two
things. First, he gave up his whole life to
be a believer in Jesus. If there had been
a division among the people of Capernaum,
and thousands of them had hated Christ,
this man would still have stood on His side.
He believed in the Lord. This is what must
take place with us. Let us go forward with
our trust in the living Christ, knowing that
He will keep us. Then we will get grace
to carry the life of Christ into our whole
conduct, into all our walk and conversation. The faith that rests in Jesus is the
faith that trusts all to Him with all we have.
Do we not read that when God had finished
His work, and rested, it was only to begin
new work? Yes, the great work was to
be carried on—watching over and ruling His
world and His church. And is it not so with
the Lord Jesus? When He had finished His
work, He sat upon the throne to do His work
of perfecting the body through the Holy
Spirit. And now, the Holy Spirit is carrying
on that blessed work, teaching us to rest
in Christ and in the strength of that rest
to go on, and to cover our whole life with
the power, and the obedience, and the will,
and the likeness of the Lord Jesus. The nobleman gave up his whole life to be a believer in Christ. From that day it was a
believer in Jesus who walked about the

streets of Capernaum; not only a man who could say, "Once He helped me," but, "I believe in Him with my whole life." Let that be so with us everywhere; let Christ be the one object of our trust.

One more thought: He believed with his whole house. That was triumphant faith. He took up his position as a believer in Christ, and gathered his wife, his children, his servants together and laid them at the feet of Christ. And if you want power in your own house, if you want power in your Bible class, if you want power in your social circle, if you want power to influence the nation, and if you want power to influence the Church of Christ, see where it begins. Come into contact with Jesus in this rest of faith that accepts His life fully, that trusts Him fully, and the power will come by faith to overcome the world, by faith to bless others, by faith to live a life to the glory of God. Go thy way, thy soul liveth; for it is Jesus Christ who liveth within you. Go thy way; be not trembling and fearful, but *rest in the word and the power of the Son of God.* "Lo, I am with you alway." Go thy way, with the heart open to welcome Him and believing He has come in. Surely we have not prayed in vain. Christ has listened to the yearnings of our hearts and has entered in. Let us go our way quietly, restfully, full of praise, and joy, and trust; ever hearing the words of our Master, "Go thy way, thy soul liveth"; and ever saying, "I have trusted Christ to reveal His abundant life in my soul. By His grace I will wait upon Him to fulfill His promise." Amen.

## 12

## The Source of Power in Prayer

*Romans 8:26-27—Likewise the Spirit also helpeth our infirmities: for we know not what we should pray for as we ought: but the Spirit itself maketh intercession for us with groanings which cannot be uttered. And he that searcheth the hearts knoweth what is the mind of the Spirit, because he maketh intercession for the saints according to the will of God.*

Here we have the teaching of God regarding the help the Holy Spirit will give us in prayer. The first half of this chapter is of much importance in connection with the teaching of God's Word regarding the Spirit. In Romans 6 we read about being dead to sin and alive to God, and in Romans 7, about being dead to the law and married to Christ, and also about the impotency of the unregenerate man to do God's will. This is only a preparation to show us how helpless we are. Then in the eighth chapter comes the blessed work of the Spirit, expressed chiefly in the following words, "The Spirit hath made us free from the law of sin and death." The Spirit makes us free from the power of sin, and teaches and leads us so that we walk after the Spirit. In our inner disposition we may become spiritually minded and enabled to mortify the deeds of the body. The Holy Spirit helps our infirmities. Prayer is the most necessary thing in the spiritual life. Yet we do not know how to pray nor what to pray for as we ought. The Spirit, Paul tells us, prays with groanings unutterable. And again he tells us that we ourselves often do not know what the Spirit is doing within us, but there is one, God, who searches the hearts.

Words often reveal my thoughts and my wishes, but not what is deep in my heart. But God comes and searches my heart, and finds deep down, hidden, what I cannot see and what was to me an unutterable longing.

Powerful prayer! The confession of ignorance! Ah, friends, I am often afraid for myself as a minister that I pray too easily. I have been praying for these forty or fifty years and it becomes as far as man is concerned, an easy thing to pray. We all have been taught to pray, and when we are called upon we can pray, but it gets far too easy, and I am afraid that often we think we are praying when there is little real prayer.

Now if we are to have the praying of
the Holy Ghost in us, one thing is needed:
we must begin by feeling, "I cannot pray."
When a man breaks down and cannot pray,
and there is a fire burning in his heart,
and a burden resting upon him, there is
something drawing him to God. "I know
not what to pray"—oh, blessed ignorance!
We are not ignorant enough. Abraham went
out not knowing whither he went. In that
there was an element of ignorance and an
element of faith. Jesus said to His disciples when they came with their prayer
for the throne, "You know not what you
ask." Paul says, "No man knoweth the
things of God but the Spirit of God." You
say, "If I am not to pray the old prayers
I learned from my mother or from my pro-
fessor in college or from my experience
yesterday and the day before, what am I
to pray?" I answer, pray new prayers;
rise higher into the riches of God. You must
begin to feel your ignorance. You know
what we think of a student who goes to
college fancying he knows everything. He
will not learn much. Sir Isaac Newton said,
"I do not know what I may appear to the
world; but to myself I seem to have been
only like a boy playing on the seashore and
diverting myself in now and then finding
a smoother pebble or a prettier shell than

ordinary, whilst the great ocean of truth lay all undiscovered before me."

When I see a man who cannot pray glibly and smoothly and readily, I say that is a mark of the Holy Spirit. When he begins in his prayers to say, "Oh, God, I want more, I want to be led deeper in. I have prayed for the heathen, but I want to feel the burden of the heathen in a new way," it is an indication of the presence of the Holy Spirit. I tell you, beloved, if you will take time and let God lay the burden of the heathen heavier upon you until you begin to feel, "I have never prayed," it will be the most blessed thing in your life.

And so with regard to the church: We want to take up our position as members of the Church of Christ in this land, and as belonging to that great body, to say, "Lord God, is there nothing that can be done to bless the church of this land and to revive it and bring it out of its worldliness and out of its feebleness?" We may confer together and conclude faithlessly, "No, we do not know what is to be done; we have no influence and power over all these ministers and their churches." But on the other hand, how blessed to come to God and say, "Lord, we know not what to ask. Thou knowest what to grant." The Holy Spirit could pray a hundredfold more in us if we were only conscious of our ignorance, because we would then feel our dependence upon Him.

May God teach us our ignorance in prayer and our impotence and bring us to say, "Lord, we cannot pray; we do not know what prayer is." Of course some of us do know in a measure what prayer is, and we thank God for what he has been to us in answer to prayer; but oh, it is only a little beginning compared to what the Holy Spirit of God teaches.

Here is the first thought: our ignorance. "We know not what we should pray for as we ought"; but "the Spirit itself maketh intercession for us with groanings which cannot be uttered." We often hear about the work of God the Father and the Son and the Holy Ghost in working out and completing the great redemption. We know that when God worked in the creation of the world, He was not weary, and yet we read that wonderful expression in the book of Exodus about the Sabbath day, "God rested and was refreshed." He was refreshed; the Sabbath day was a refreshment to Him.

God had to work and Christ had to work. Now the Holy Spirit works, and His secret working place, the place where all work must begin, is in the heart where He comes to teach a man how to pray. When a man begins to get an insight into that which is needed and that which is promised and that which God waits to perform, he feels it to be beyond his conception. Then is the time he will be ready to say, "I cannot limit the holy one of Israel by my thoughts. I give myself up in the faith that the Holy Spirit can be praying for me with groanings, with longings, that cannot be expressed." Apply that to your prayers.

There are different phases of prayer. There is worship, when a man just bows down to adore the great God. We do not take time to worship. We need to worship in secret, just to get ourselves face to face with the everlasting God that He may overshadow us and cover us and fill us with His love and His glory. It is the Holy Spirit who can work in us such a yearning that we will give up our pleasures and even part of our business that we may the oftener meet our God.

The next phase of prayer is fellowship. In prayer there is not only the worship of a king, but fellowship as of a child with God. Christians take far too little time in fellowship. They think prayer is just coming with their petitions. If Christ is to make me what I am to be, I must tarry in fellowship with God. If God is to let His love

enter in and shine and burn through my
heart, I must take time to be with Him.
The smith puts his rod of iron into the fire.
If he leaves it there but a short time it
does not become red hot. He may take it
out to do something with it and after a time
put it back again for a few minutes, but
this time it does not become red hot. In
the course of the day he may put the rod
into the fire a great many times and leave
it there two or three minutes each time,
but it never becomes thoroughly heated.
If he takes time and leaves the rod ten
or fifteen minutes in the fire the whole iron
will become red hot with the heat that is
in the fire.

So it is with us, if we are to get the
fire of God's holiness and love and power
we must take more time with God in fellowship. That was what gave men like
Abraham and Moses their strength. They
were men who were separated to a fellowship with God, and the living God made
them strong. Oh, if we did but realize what
prayer can do!

Another very important phase of prayer
is intercession. What a work God has set
open for those who are His priests—intercessors! We find a wonderful expression in
the prophecy of Isaiah. God says, "Let him
take hold of me"; and again, "There is

none that stirreth up himself to take hold
of thee." In other passages God refers to
the intercessors for Israel. Have you ever
taken hold of God? Thank God, some of
us have. But oh, friends, representatives
of the Church of Christ in the United States,
if God were to show us how much there
is of intense prayer for a revival through
the church, how much of sincere confession
of the sins of the church, how much of pleading with God and giving Him no rest till
He make Jerusalem a glory in the earth,
I think we should all be ashamed. We need
to give up our hearts to the Holy Spirit,
that He may pray for us and in us with
groanings that cannot be uttered.

What am I to do if I am to have this
Holy Spirit within me? The Spirit wants
time and room in the heart; He wants the
whole being. He wants all my interest and
influence going out for the honor and the
glory of God; He wants me to give myself up. Beloved friend, you do not know
what you could do if you would give yourself up to intercession. It is a work that
a sick one lying on a bed year by year
may do in power. It is a work that a poor
one who has hardly a penny to give to a
missionary society can do day by day. It
is a work that a young girl who is in her
father's house and has to help in the house-

keeping can do by the Holy Spirit. People often ask: What does the church of our day do to reach the masses? They ask, though they ask it tremblingly, for they feel so helpless: What can we do against the materialism and infidelity in places like London and Berlin and New York and Paris? We have given it up as hopeless. Ah, if men and women could be called out to band themselves together to take hold upon God! I am not speaking of any prayer union or any prayer time statedly set apart, but if the Spirit could find men and women who would give up their lives to cry to God, the Spirit would most surely come. It is not selfishness and it is not mere happiness that we seek when we talk about the peace and the rest and the blessing Christ can give. God wants us, Christ wants us, because He has to do a work; the work of Calvary is to be done in our hearts, we are to sacrifice our lives to pleading with God for men. Oh, let us yield ourselves day by day and ask God that it may please Him to let His Holy Spirit work in us.

Then comes the last thought, that God himself comes to look with complacency upon the attitude of His child. Perhaps that poor man does not know that he is praying; perhaps he is ashamed of his prayers. So much the better. Perhaps he feels burdened

and restless, but God hears, God discovers
what is the mind of the Spirit and will answer. Oh, think of this wonderful mystery,
God the Father on the throne ready to grant
unto us His blessings according to the riches
of His glory. Christ the almighty high priest
pleading day and night. His whole person
is one intercession, and there goes up from
Him without ceasing the pleading to the
Father, "Bless thy church," and the answer
comes from the Father to the Son, and from
the Son down to the church, and if it does
not reach us, it is because our hearts are
closed.

Let us open and enlarge our hearts and
say to God, "Oh, that I might be a priest,
to enter God's presence continually and to
take hold of God and to bring down a blessing to my perishing fellowmen!" God longs
to find the intercession of Jesus reflected
in the hearts of His children, and where
He finds it, it is a delight. And He who
searches the hearts knows the mind of the
Spirit, because he prays for the saints according to the will of God. Someone has
said that the words "for the saints" means
the spirit of praise in the believer for the
saints throughout the world. God's word
continually comes to us to pray for all and
not to be content with ourselves. Think upon
the hundreds of church members in this

land, multitudes unconverted, multitudes just converted, but yet worldly and careless. Think of the thousands of nominal Christians—Christians in name, but robbing God! And can we be happy? If we bear the burden of souls, can we have this peace and joy? God gives you peace and joy with no other object than that you should be strong to bear the burden of souls in the joy of Christ's salvation.

We do not wish to say, "I am trying to be as holy as I can. What have I to do with those worldly people about me?" If there is a terrible disease in my hand, my body cannot say, "I have nothing to do with it." When the people had sinned, Ezra rent his garments and bowed in the dust and made confession. He repented on the part of the people. And Nehemiah, when the nation sinned, made confession and cast himself before God, deploring their disobedience to the God of their fathers. Daniel did the very same. And think you that we as believers have not a great work to do? Suppose each of us were persons without a single sin—just suppose it. Could we then make confession? Look at Christ, without sin! He went down into the waters of baptism with sinners. He made himself one with them. God has spoken to us to ask us if we realize what we are. He now asks us whether we belong to the church of this land, whether we have borne the burden of sin around us. Let us go to God and may He by the Holy Spirit fill our hearts with unutterable sorrow at the state of the church, and may God give us grace to mourn before Him. And when we begin to confess the sins of the church, we will begin to feel our own sins as never before. In five of the epistles to the seven churches in Asia the keynote was "Repent"; there was to be no idea of overcoming and getting a blessing unless they repented. Let us on behalf of the Church of Christ repent, and God will give us courage to feel that He will revive His work.

## 13

## That God May Be All in All

*I Corinthians 15:24-28—Then cometh the end, when he shall have delivered up the kingdom to God, even the Father; when he shall have put down all rule, and all authority and power. For he must reign till he hath put all enemies under his feet. The last enemy that shall be destroyed is death. For he hath put all things under his feet. But when he saith all things are put under him, it is manifest that he is excepted, which did put all things under him. And when all things shall be subdued unto him, then shall the Son also himself be subject unto him, that God may be all in all.*

This will be the grand conclusion of the great drama of the world's history and of Christ's redemption. There will come a day —the glory is such we can form no conception of it, the mystery is so deep we cannot realize it—when the Son shall deliver up the kingdom that the Father gave Him and which He won with His blood and established and perfected from the throne of His glory. "He shall deliver up the kingdom unto the Father." The Son himself shall be subject also unto the Father "that God may be all in all." I cannot understand it—the ever blessed Son equal with God, from eternity and through eternity; the ever blessed Son on the throne shall be subject unto the Father; and in some way utterly beyond our comprehension, it shall then be made manifest, as never before, that God is all in all. It is this that Christ has been working for; it is this that He is working for today in us; it is this that He thought it worthwhile to give His blood for; it is this that His heart is longing for in each of us. This is the very essence and glory of Christianity: "that God may be all in all."

And now, if this is what fills the heart of Christ; if this expresses the one end of the work of Christ, then, if I want to have the spirit of Christ in me, the motto of my life must be: Everything made subject and swallowed up in Him "that God may be all in all." What a triumph it would be if the church were fighting really with that banner floating over her! What a life ours could be if that were really our banner! To serve God fully, wholly, only, to have Him all in all! How it would ennoble and enlarge and stimulate our whole being! I am working, I am fighting, "that God may be all in all"; that the day of glory may be hastened. I am praying, and the Holy Spirit makes His wrestling in me with unutterable longing, "that God may be all in all." Would that we Christians realized with what a grand cause we are working and praying; that we had some conception of the kingdom we are partakers of, and what a manifestation of God we are preparing for.

To illustrate what a grand thing it is to belong to the Kingdom of God and to the glorious Church of Christ on earth, John McNeill tells how when he was a boy twelve years of age, working on a railway line and earning the grand wages of six shillings a week, he used to go home to his mother and sisters, who thought no end of their little Johnnie, and delight them by telling of the position he had. He would say with great pride, "Oh, our company—it has so many thousands of pounds passing through its hands every year; it carries so many hundreds of thousands of passengers every year; and it has so many miles of railway and so many engines and carriages; it has so many thousands in its employ!" And the mother and the sisters had great pride in him because he was a partner in such an important business.

Christians, if we would only rouse our-

selves to believe that we belong to the kingdom that Christ is preparing to deliver up
to the Father that God may be all in all,
how the glory would fill our hearts and expel everything mean, and low, and earthly!
How we should be borne along in this
blessed faith! I am living for this: that
Christ may have the kingdom to deliver
to the Father. I am living for this, and I
will one day see Him made subject to the
Father, and then God will be all in all. I
am living for Him, and I shall be there not
only as a witness, but I will have a part
in it all. The kingdom delivered up, the Son
made subject, and God all in all! I shall
have a part in it and in adoring worship
share the glory and the blessedness.

Let us take this home to our hearts that
it may rule in our lives—this one thought,
this one faith, this one aim, this one joy:
Christ lived and died and reigns; I live and
die and in His power I reign only for this
one thing, "that God may be all in all."
Let it possess our whole heart and life. How
can we do this? It is a serious question
to which I wish to give you a few simple
answers. And I say, first of all, "Allow God
to take His place in your heart and life."
Luther often said to people when they came
troubling him about difficulties, "Do let
God be God." Oh, give God His place. And

what is that place? "That God may be all in all." Let God be all in all every day, from morning to evening. God to rule and I to obey. Ah, the blessedness of saying, "God and I!" What a privilege that I have such a partner! God first, and then I! And yet there might be secret self-exaltation in associating God with myself.

I find in the Bible a more precious word still. It is, "God and not I." It is not, "God first, and I second." God is all and I am nothing. Paul said, "I labored more abundantly than they all; though I be nothing." Let us try to give God His place—begin in our closet, in our worship, in our prayer. The power of prayer depends almost entirely upon our apprehension of who it is with whom we speak. It is of the greatest consequence, if we have but half an hour in which to pray, that we take time to get a sight of this great God—in His power, in His love, in His nearness—just waiting to bless us. This is of far more consequence than spending the whole half hour in pouring out numberless petitions and pleading numberless promises. The great thing is to feel that we are putting our supplications into the bosom of omnipotent Love. Before and above everything, let us take time ere we pray to realize the glory and presence of God. Give God His place

in every prayer. I say, allow God to have
His place. I cannot give God His place upon
the throne (in a certain sense I can, and
I ought to try). The great thing, however,
is for me to feel that I cannot realize what
that place is, but God will increasingly reveal himself and the place He holds. How
do I know anything about the sun? Because the sun shines and in its light I see
what the sun is. The sun is its own evidence.
No philosopher could have told me about
the sun if the sun did not shine. No power
of meditation and thought can grasp the
presence of God. Be quiet, and trusting, and
resting, and the everlasting God will shine
into your heart, and will reveal himself.
And then, just as naturally as I enjoy the
light of the sun, and as naturally as I look
upon the pages of a book knowing that I
can see the letters because the light shines;
just as naturally will God reveal himself
to the waiting soul and make His presence
a reality. God will take His place as God
in the presence of His child, so that absolutely and actually the chief thing in the
child's heart shall be: "God is here, God
makes himself known."

Beloved, is not this what you long for—
that God shall take a place that He has
never had; and that God shall come to you
in a nearness that you have never felt yet;

and, above all, that God shall come to you in an abiding and unbroken fellowship? God is able to take His place before you all the day. I repeat what I have referred to before, because God has taught me a lesson by it: As God made the light of the sun so soft, sweet, bright, universal, and unceasing, that it never costs me a minute's trouble to enjoy it; even so, and far more real than the light shining upon me, the nearness of my God can be revealed to me as my abiding portion. Let us all pray "that God may be all in all" in our everyday life.

"That God may be all in all," I must not only allow Him to take His place, but secondly, I must accept His will in everything. I must accept His will in every providence. Whether it be a Judas that betrays, or whether it be a Pilate in his indifference who gives me up to the enemy; whatever the trouble, or temptation, or vexation, or worry, that comes, I must see God in it and accept it as God's will to me. Trouble of any sort that comes to me is God's will for me. It is not God's will that men should do the wrong, but it is God's will that they should be in circumstances of trial. There is never a trial that comes to us but it is God's will for us, and if we learn to see God in it, then we bid it welcome.

Suppose away in South Africa there is a woman whose husband has gone on a long journey into the interior. He is to be away for months from all posts. The wife is anxious to receive news. In weeks she has had no letter or tidings from him. One day as she stands in her door, there comes a great, savage Kafir. He is frightful in appearance, and carries his spears and shield. The woman is alarmed and rushes into the house and closes the door. He comes and knocks at the door, and she is in terror. She sends her servant, who comes back and says, "The man says he must see you." She goes, all affrighted. He takes out an old newspaper. He has come a month's journey on foot from her husband, and inside the dirty newspaper is a letter from her husband, telling her of his welfare. How that wife delights in that letter! She forgets the face that has terrified her. And now as weeks are passing away again, how she begins to long for that ugly Kafir messenger! After long waiting he comes again, and this time she rushes out to meet him because he is the messenger that comes from her beloved husband, and she knows that with all his repelling exterior, he is the bearer of a message of love.

Beloved, have you learned to look at tribulation and vexation and disappointment as the dark, savage-looking messenger with a spear in his hand that comes straight from Jesus? Have you learned to say, "There is never a trouble and never a hurt by which my heart is touched or even pierced, but it comes from Jesus, and brings a message of love"? Will you not learn to say from today, "Welcome every trial, for it comes from God"? If you want God to be all in all, you must see and meet God in every providence. Oh, learn to accept God's will in everything! Come, learn to say of every trial, without exception, "It is my Father who sent it. I accept it as His messenger," and nothing in earth or hell can separate you from God.

If God is to be all in all in your heart and life, I say not only, allow Him to take His place and accept all His will, but, thirdly, *trust in His power.* Dear friends, it is "God who *worketh in you to will and to do* according to his good pleasure." It is "the God of peace," according to another passage, "who perfects you in every good thing to do His will, *working in you* that which is well-pleasing in his sight." You complain of weakness, of feebleness, of emptiness. Never mind; that is what you are made for—to be an emptied vessel in which God can put His fullness and His strength. Do learn the lesson. I know it is not easy. Long after Paul had been an apostle, the Lord Jesus had to come in a very special way to teach him to say, "I do gladly glory in my infirmities." Paul was in danger of being exalted, owing to the revelations from heaven, and Jesus sent him a thorn in the flesh—yes, Jesus sent it—a messenger of Satan—to buffet him. Paul prayed, and struggled, and wanted to get rid of it. And Jesus came to him, and said, "It is my doing that you may not be free from that. You need it. I will bless you wonderfully in it." Paul's life was changed from that moment in this one respect, and he said, "I never knew it so before; from henceforth I glory in my infirmities; for when I am weak, then am I strong."

Do you indeed desire God to be all in all? Learn to glory in your weakness. Take time to say every day as you bow before God, "The almighty power of God that works in the sun, the moon, and the stars, and the flowers is working in me. It is as sure as that I live. The almighty power of God is working in me. I only need to get down and be quiet. I need to be more submissive and surrendered to His will. I need to be more trustful and to allow God to do with me what He will." Let God have His way with you. Let Him work and He will work mightily. The deepest quietness

has often been proved to be the inspiration
for the highest action. It has been seen in
the experience of many of God's saints, and
it is just the experience we need—that in
the quietness of surrender and faith, God's
working has been made manifest.

Fourthly: If God is to be all in all, sacrifice everything for His kingdom and glory.
"That God may be all in all." This is such
a noble, glorious, holy aim that Christ said,
"For this I will give my life. For this I
will give my all, even to the death of the
cross. For this I will give myself." If it
was worth that to Christ, is it worth less
to you? If one had asked Jesus of Nazareth,
"What is it Thou hast a body for; what
is to Thee the highest use of the body?"
He would have said, "The use and the glory
of my body is that I can give it a sacrifice
to God. That is everything." What is the
use of having a mind, of having money,
of having children? That I can give them
to God, for God must be all in all in everything.

I pray God that He may give us such
a sight of His kingdom and His glory that
everything else may disappear. Then, if you
had ten thousand lives, you would say,
"This is the beauty and the worth of life,
'that God may be all in all' to me, and
that I may prove to men that God is more

than everything, that life is worth living only as it is given to God to fill." Do let us sacrifice everything for His kingdom and glory. Begin to live day by day with the prayer, "My God, I am given up to Thee. Be Thou my all in all." You say, "Am I able to realize that?" Yes, in this way: Let the Holy Spirit dwell in you; let the Holy Spirit burn in you as a fire with unutterable groanings, crying unto God, himself to reveal His presence and His will in you. In the eighth of Romans, Paul spoke about the groanings of the whole creation. And what is the whole creation groaning for? For the redemption, the glorious liberty of the children of God. And I am persuaded that was what Paul meant when he spoke of the groanings of the Holy Spirit —the unutterable groanings for the coming time of glory when God should be all in all.

Christians, sacrifice your time; sacrifice your interests; sacrifice your heart's best powers in praying and desiring and crying that "God may be all in all."

And lastly: If God is to be all in all, wait continually on Him all the day. My first point had reference to giving God His place; but I want to bring this out more pointedly in conclusion. Wait continually on God all the day. If you are to do that you must live always in His presence. That is what we have been redeemed for. Do we not read in the Epistle to the Hebrews, "Let us draw near within the veil, through the blood, where the high priest is"? The holy place in which we are to live in the heavens is the immediate presence of God. The abiding presence of God is certainly the heritage of every child of God, as sure as the sun shines. The Father never hides His face from His child. Sin hides it, and unbelief hides it, but the Father lets His love shine all day on the face of His children. The sun is shining day and night. Your sun shall never go down. Begin to seek for this. Come and live in the presence of God. There is indeed an abiding place in His presence, in the secret of His pavilion, of which someone has sung very beautifully:

> With me, wheresoe'er I wander,
>     That great Presence goes;
> That unutterable gladness,
>     Undisturbed repose.

> Everywhere, the blessed stillness
>     Of that Holy Place;
> Stillness of the love that worships,
>     Dumb before His face.

This is the portion of those to whom the prayer is granted: "One thing have I desired of the Lord, and that will I seek after; that I may dwell all my days in the house

of the Lord; to behold the beauty of the
Lord, and to inquire in his temple." "In
the secret of His pavilion He hideth me."
God himself will take you up and keep you
there, so that all your work shall be done
in God.

Beloved, wait continually upon God.
You cannot do this unless you are in His
presence. You must live in His presence.
Then the blessed habit of waiting upon God
will be learned. The real difficulty of getting
to the point of real waiting upon God is
because most Christians have not sought
to realize the nearness of God and to give
God the first place. But let us strive after
this: let us trust God to give it to us by
His grace; let us wait on God all the day.
"My eyes," says one, "are ever towards
Thee." Wait upon God for guidance, and
God, if you wait much upon Him, will lead
you up into new power for His service, into
new gladness in His fellowship. He will lead
you out into a larger trust in Him. He will
prepare you to expect new things from Him.
Beloved, there is no knowing what God will
do for a man who is utterly given up to
Him. Praise His name! Let each one of us
say, "May my life be to live and die, to
labor and to pray continually for this one
thing: that in me, and around me and in

the church—that throughout the world *God may be all in all.*"

A little seed is the beginning of a great tree. A mustard seed becomes a tree in which the birds of the air can nestle. That great day of which the text speaks, when Christ himself shall be subject to the Father, and deliver up the kingdom to the Father, and God shall be all in all—that is the great tree of the Kingdom of God reaching its perfect consummation and glory. Oh, let us take the seed of that glory into our hearts and let us bow in lowly surrender and submission, saying "Amen, Lord; this be my one thought. This be my life—to speak and to work, to pray and to exist only that others may be brought to know Him too. This be my life—to yield myself to the unutterable yearnings of the Holy Spirit that I may not rest, but ever keep my eye on that day—the day of glory, when in very deed God shall be all in all."

God help every one of us. God help us all to yield ourselves to Him, and to Christ, and to make it our everyday life, for His name's sake. Amen.